D1594096

WRITING IN ANTHROPOLOGY

# BRIEF GUIDES TO
# WRITING IN THE DISCIPLINES

Edited by
THOMAS DEANS, *University of Connecticut*
MYA POE, *Northeast University*

Although writing-intensive courses across the disciplines are now common at many colleges and universities, few books meet the precise needs of those offerings. These books do. Compact, candid, and practical, the *Brief Guides to Writing in the Disciplines* deliver experience-tested lessons and essential writing resources for those navigating fields ranging from Biology and Engineering to Music and Political Science.

Authored by experts in the field who also have knack for teaching, these books introduce students to discipline-specific writing habits that seem natural to insiders but still register as opaque to those new to a major or to specialized research. Each volume offers key writing strategies backed by crisp explanations and examples; each anticipates the missteps that even bright newcomers to a specialized discourse typically make; and each addresses the irksome details that faculty get tired of marking up in student papers.

For faculty accustomed to teaching their own subject matter but not writing, these books provide a handy vocabulary for communicating what good academic writing is and how to achieve it. Most of us learn to write through trial and error, often over many years, but struggle to impart those habits of thinking and writing to our students. The *Brief Guides to Writing in the Disciplines* make both the central lessons and the field-specific subtleties of writing explicit and accessible.

These versatile books will be immediately useful for writing-intensive courses but should also prove an ongoing resource for students as they move through more advanced courses, on to capstone research experiences, and even into their graduate studies and careers.

# OTHER AVAILABLE TITLES IN THIS SERIES INCLUDE:

**Writing in Engineering:** *A Brief Guide*

Robert Irish
(ISBN: 9780199343553)

**Writing in Political Science:** *A Brief Guide*

Mika LaVaque-Manty and Danielle LaVaque-Manty
(ISBN: 9780190203931)

**Writing in Nursing:** *A Brief Guide*

Thomas Lawrence Long and Cheryl Tatano Beck
(ISBN: 9780190202231)

**Writing in Sociology:** *A Brief Guide*

Cary Moskovitz and Lynn Smith-Lovin
(ISBN: 9780190203924)

**Writing in Biology:** *A Brief Guide*

Leslie Ann Roldan and Mary-Lou Pardue
(ISBN: 9780199342716)

# WRITING IN ANTHROPOLOGY

## A BRIEF GUIDE

Shan-Estelle Brown

ROLLINS COLLEGE

New York     Oxford
Oxford University Press

Oxford University Press is a department of the University of Oxford.
It furthers the University's objective of excellence in research, scholarship,
and education by publishing worldwide. Oxford is a registered trade mark
of Oxford University Press in the UK and certain other countries.

Published in the United States of America by Oxford University Press
198 Madison Avenue, New York, NY 10016, United States of America.

For titles covered by Section 112 of the US Higher Education
Opportunity Act, please visit www.oup.com/us/he for the
latest information about pricing and alternate formats.

**Library of Congress Cataloging-in-Publication Data**

Names: Brown, Shan-Estelle, author.
Title: Writing in anthropology : a brief guide / Shan-Estelle Brown, Rollins
    College.
Description: New York : Oxford University Press, [2017] | Series: Brief
    guides to writing in the disciplines
Identifiers: LCCN 2016040839
Subjects: LCSH: Anthropology--Authorship. | Ethnology--Authorship. |
    Anthropology--Research. | Ethnology--Research.
Classification: LCC GN307.7 .B76 2017 | DDC 808.06/63--dc23 LC record
    available at https://lccn.loc.gov/2016040839

9 8 7 6 5 4 3 2 1

Printed by LSC Communications, United States of America

# BRIEF CONTENTS

# TABLE OF CONTENTS

# PREFACE

This book is an attempt to solve a problem: Student writers in anthropology courses are often confused and frustrated when it comes to writing a successful paper. It happens to non-majors and majors alike. No matter the discipline, anthropologists discuss writing and style with other professionals, but there has been no compact, practical writing guide that meets the needs of undergraduates and beginning graduate students. This book presents strategies for writing anthropologically about the world, as well as sentence-level style tips for effective prose. These are all expectations that anthropology instructors think are important but are often left unspoken.

While I am a medical anthropologist, I bring examples from across all subdisciplines in anthropology, trying not to play favorites. Meanwhile, I have tried to balance those practical models with important theoretical and methodological discussions.

This book is intended to be accessible enough to be used in introductory anthropology courses yet robust enough to serve upper-level undergraduates (and even early graduate students) as they approach assignments that range from brief essays to research papers. Chapter 1 describes the different types of writing that professional anthropologists do and the expectations that anthropology instructors place on student writing, helping students to see their writing in a broader context, and especially as adding to our existing understanding about what it means to be human. Introductory students will find Chapter 2 especially useful, as it offers tips for the shorter assignments they are likely to encounter. Chapter 3 is designed to support courses that include field-based components; it demystifies observation assignments, participant-observation assignments, writing basic fieldnotes, and writing in a reflexive way. Chapters 4 and 5 speak to literature reviews and research papers and will prove especially apt for writing-intensive courses. Chapter 6 not only addresses the most common style and usage issues in writing generally but also attends to style conventions specific to anthropology. The final chapter delivers not only a brief guide to citing sources but also those hard-to-teach strategies for integrating source material into one's own writing.

# ABOUT THE AUTHOR

SHAN-ESTELLE BROWN is a medical anthropologist and assistant professor of anthropology at Rollins College. Previously, she was a postdoctoral researcher in the AIDS Program at Yale School of Medicine. She has taught writing-intensive Anthropology and English composition courses at the university and community college levels. She also worked for four years at the University of Connecticut Writing Center, tutoring hundreds of undergraduate students for anthropology and other coursework, conducting research on composition and writing centers, and developing programs to support instructors of writing-intensive classes. She holds a doctorate in Anthropology from the University of Connecticut, a Master of Arts in English from Old Dominion University, and a Bachelor of Arts in Humanities from Yale University.

# ACKNOWLEDGMENTS

I would like to thank my editors Tom Deans and Mya Poe for their immeasurably helpful and timely comments and suggestions. Thank you also to the Oxford University Press team of editors and copywriters and to Jenneffer Sixkiller, MLIS, for developing the index; I've never seen my writing look better. Special thanks also goes to the student writers at the University of Connecticut and Quinebaug Valley Community College whose work appears here—thank you for letting me share my passions for anthropology and writing with you. I am very grateful for those who reviewed the manuscript: Jennifer Birch, University of Georgia; Brian F. Codding, University of Utah; Joseph E. Diamond, SUNY New Paltz; Molly Doane, University of Illinois at Chicago; Joseph Hankins, University of California, San Diego; Leslie A. Knapp, University of Utah; Shaylih Muehlmann, University of British Columbia; Edmund Searles, Bucknell University; and Michael J. Sheridan, Middlebury College. I also thank my family and friends for cheering me on and for bearing with me when it seemed like agony to just finish a sentence. I've become a stronger writer and more confident anthropologist after having gone through this process.

# THINKING AND WRITING
# LIKE AN ANTHROPOLOGIST

At the University of Chicago so long ago, I had to select
a specialty from these five fields in anthropology:
archaeology, cultural anthropology, ethnology,
linguistics, and physical anthropology. I chose cultural
anthropology, since it offered the greatest opportunity
to write high-minded balderdash.

—Kurt Vonnegut (1981, 222) in his
autobiography *Palm Sunday*

Kurt Vonnegut was joking, of course, when he winked at
cultural anthropology as a discipline where he could write
"balderdash"—nonsense—but we understand what he meant,
because anthropological writing can be bewildering. In an
effort to "make the strange familiar and the familiar strange,"
anthropologists write to confront the way readers think
about what it means to be human. Anthropologists challenge
our everyday assumptions about society and the way it is
constructed. Because of these complexities, writing effectively
about human societies can be difficult or even bewildering.

Anthropology is the study of all things concerning humans.
Two features that distinguish anthropology from other social
sciences are, as James Lett [3] argues, its focus on *culture* and its

negotiation of the *emic/etic distinction*—that is, conducting and understanding human research from the perspective of either a cultural insider (*emic*) or outsider (*etic*). As a consequence, anthropology is a holistic discipline (i.e., everything is anthropological) as well as a comparative discipline. Lett (1987, 61–62) reflects on just how broad the field is and how that provokes difficult questions:

> Most introductory textbooks in anthropology describe the discipline as "holistic" and "comparative". The anthropological perspective is ***holistic*** because it tries to examine the whole of human experience. That is, unlike political scientists, sociologists, or economists, anthropologists try to look beyond political, social, or economic behavior to the interplay among all these factors of human life and to see the connections between them. Of course, anthropologists attempt to incorporate many more factors into their "holistic" analyses, including biological, ecological, linguistic, historical, and ideological variables. The anthropological perspective is ***comparative*** because it seeks its information and tests its explanations among all of the prehistorical, historical, and contemporary cultures to which anthropologists have access.

Although people have been thinking and writing about the human experience for thousands of years, it was not until 1896 that the first academic department of anthropology in the United States was founded—that one by Franz Boas at Columbia University. Since then, anthropology has flourished, but not without tensions, such as whether or not anthropology counts as a science, how objectivity and subjectivity figure in research, how to deal with the field's colonial legacy and other critiques of early anthropologists who established the field, and to what extent anthropology "owns" the study of culture.

Given that even seasoned anthropologists argue vigorously about the boundaries and nature of their field, it is no wonder that with each new anthropology course, students are anxious about writing expectations. Clifford and Marcus's [5] influential book *Writing Culture* sparked numerous debates among professional anthropologists about terms like *reflexivity, objectivity,* and *authority* in ethnographic writing, but these complexities may not be the most practical starting place for students to understand anthropological writing. Instead, students typically wonder what kind or genre of writing their instructor wants them to do, what particular writing pet peeves he or she has, and what skills they can carry over from previous classes. In their first assignments, some students resort to the five-paragraph essay format (or some close cousin of it) because that feels safe. In an attempt to sound professional, students also often force anthropological terms into their prose, leaving sentences looking like overstuffed suitcases. Over time—and through lots of reading, studying, drafting, and revising—students get better at seeing the world through an anthropological lens and writing in a register that makes their anthropology professors nod in affirmation. The process is neither quick nor easy. It takes concerted attention and some determination. It demands practice and involves mistakes. Such struggles are natural, even anthropological. Over time, you become more and more adept at interpreting the disciplinary culture and navigating your way.

Learning to write like an anthropologist can be daunting, but you can speed up that process if, like an anthropologist, you come to recognize the values, patterns, and assumptions in the field. If you are an undergraduate student in anthropology, this book is designed to help you understand how anthropologists think, how research and writing differ across the subfields, how to adopt effective strategies for writing your papers, and how to follow anthropology norms regarding citation and style. If you are a new graduate student, you may likewise find the book helpful, especially if you did not major in anthropology in college. This book demystifies the expectations for writing in anthropology and provides you with pragmatic strategies to help you meet—perhaps even exceed— those expectations. And that's no balderdash.

## Instead of Anthropology, Think Anthropologies

Anthropologists are as diverse as the people and places they study. At academic conferences, one index of this diversity is clothing: the corporate anthropologists wear suits; the academics tend toward professor-like casual, albeit some with accents of their lives abroad—an interesting scarf, a fedora; a few people arrive in the full authentic dress of the indigenous people they work with. If you asked them to name what they have in common, they would probably only be able to agree that they all do *fieldwork* to understand the human experience.

But there the similarities end. Instead of a single anthropology, consider instead that there are actually many anthropologies. If you look at the program for the Annual Meeting of the American Anthropological Association, you see Anthropology of Consciousness, Anthropology of Europe, Anthropology of Food and Nutrition, Anthropology of North America, Anthropology of Religion, and the Anthropology of Work, just to name a few.

Anthropology began with the idea of functionalism, which viewed culture as a closed system that is the sum of its parts. Today, as anthropology has developed into a discipline with many subfields, researchers in each subfield draw upon its own theoretical traditions. For example, any anthropologist interested in the human body, power, and sexuality reads Michel Foucault. In contrast, anthropologists who consider themselves interpretivists look to Clifford Geertz and his concept of thick description. Do you study the relationship between language and society? You'd better mention Claude Lévi-Strauss. Evolutionary anthropology? Charles Darwin is only the beginning. If you hear the words "social capital" and "habitus" in class, your professor is using the framework of sociologist Pierre Bourdieu. Globalization? Look to Arjun Appadurai. If you are interested in biocultural anthropology, the relationship between culture and human biology, you would read James Bindon and William Dressler. If you study critical race theory in anthropology, Lee D. Baker's work would inform your own, and you could even go all the way back to Franz Boas, as he paved the way for understanding the social construction of race. If you were interested in feminist interpretations of anthropology, you would cite Lila Abu-Lughod. As you go further into your study of feminism you would realize there are actually several different versions of feminism; for example, black feminist anthropology [6] simultaneously challenges feminism and anthropology.

Beyond diversity in theory, there is real range in method. Let's say a biological anthropologist, a cultural anthropologist, a linguistic anthropologist, and an archaeologist all happen to see a woman sitting at a table. She picks up a pen and begins to write. Who sees what?

- A biological anthropologist would see the woman writing and want to know what's happening in the brain to make these actions happen. How did she learn to write? What were the evolutionary steps that happened in the past for humans to be able to write? How might this woman's use of the writing utensil and a notepad be similar to how chimps and bonobos use sticks as tools?

- A cultural anthropologist would want to talk to this woman to find out more about the context of her writing. What provoked or inspired her to write? And what is she writing? Who taught her to write? What's the value of writing? Would what she writes change depending on the situation?
- A linguistic anthropologist would want to know what this person is writing and why. What's her reason for choosing this medium of communication? In what language is she writing? What are the habits and norms involved in writing, and how is the act of writing affected by social factors of race, class, and gender?
- An archaeologist would think of this woman's writing as something that might be left behind. What would remain—what would be left of the paper, the writing utensil, the woman? How would any of these be preserved? How will future archaeologists interpret what this woman wrote, and would they be accurate?

Right now these theories and methods are probably alien to you. But ultimately all anthropologists need to develop a familiarity with key figures and multiple perspectives, even if, during their careers, they will be more likely to adopt one or a small set of methods. In this book I will be focusing on the habits of mind—and writing—that persist across most of the subfields most of the time, but you should at least be aware of range of specialties and know that each will have its own preferences for not just for focus and content but also for format and style.

## How Writing Happens in Anthropology

Anthropologists are perhaps best known for doing fieldwork at sites around the globe. Yet because they need to record observations, pursue grants, and publish their findings, they also spend a great deal of time writing. If you look at pictures of anthropologists in the field, most are enmeshed in the bustle of life around them, but another iconic kind of photo is the anthropologist seated, dutifully writing fieldnotes. Taking good fieldnotes is an art of its own, one beyond the scope of this book, although Chapter 3 will offer some basic advice on how to take fieldnotes for the mini-ethnographies sometimes assigned in undergraduate courses.

Anthropologists mostly—but not only—write for other anthropologists. Ethnographies and peer-reviewed research (articles and books) are considered the highest standards of academic writing in the field. Scholars also publish reviews and write grant proposals, and many have expanded into a wider variety of genres. Some have turned to auto-ethnography,

FIGURE 1.1   Margaret Mead and Gregory Bateson typing up their field notes in Papua New Guinea, 1938.

Evoking the *Indiana Jones* films, the literary magazine *McSweeney's* pokes fun at how fieldwork can sit in tension with academic writing:

> Though Dr. Jones conducts "field research" far more often than anyone else in the department, he has consistently failed to report the results of his excavations, provide any credible evidence of attending the archaeological conferences he claims to attend, or produce a single published article in any peer-reviewed journal. Someone might tell Dr. Jones that in academia "publish or perish" is the rule. (Bryan 2006)

Even while wincing at the fictionalized treasure-hunting of Indiana Jones because it traffics in thoroughly discredited notions of exoticizing "native" cultures, most anthropologists would chuckle at the truth behind the *McSweeney's* satire. Anthropologists do fieldwork, but they also need to write about their research findings.

which self-consciously blends personal narrative with traditional analysis [7]. Some mix ethnography with nonfiction [8] or poetry [9]. Some write novels [10], fiction based on field research [11], or ethnographic novels [12]. The *Temperance Brennan* series of novels by forensic anthropologist Kathy Reichs gave rise to the TV show *Bones*. Some publish in magazines such as *National Geographic, Pacific Standard,* or *The New Yorker*. Blogs allow others to share up-to-the-minute, less censored, even funny material—though material still very much informed by anthropological habits of mind. For example, *Savage Minds* (with "savage" here an ironic wink at outdated notions of the

anthropologist as discovering "primitive" or "savage" cultures)
is a group blog devoted to "doing anthropology in public."

## Genres of Anthropological Writing

Many student writing assignments are similar to the kind of
writing that professional anthropologists do, but they are
scaled down to help student writers develop specific writing
abilities, such as summarizing someone else's work, interpreting a text, or writing up the results of data analysis.

You will see Figure 1.2 reprinted—with some variations—
in Chapters 2 through 5. It is meant to orient you to the structure of common assignments. The $x$ axis represents a spectrum
of how data are obtained. The "empirical/critical'" axis maps
onto whether or not the work requires primary sources (data
collected firsthand) or secondary sources (where you work

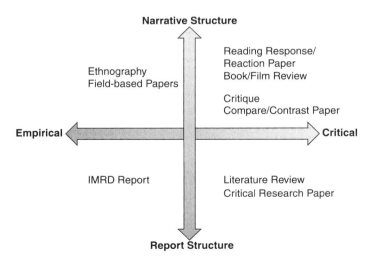

FIGURE 1.2  Common Types of Anthropological Writing in
          Relation to Their Structure and Approach to Sources.

with research that someone else has collected and interpreted). In contrast, the *y* axis represents what the written end product looks like. A professional anthropologist would recognize the axes as representing different theories. The "narrative structure" end of the axis tends toward subjectivity and interpretive and postmodern approaches, whereas the "report structure" end tends toward objectivity and positivist and classical approaches. The genres discussed in this book are plotted along these axes.

## Expectations for Anthropological Writing

The chapters that follow detail strategies for particular kinds of assignments, but you should also be aware of some overarching expectations for writers in anthropology, ones rooted in core values of the discipline. These are a big part of what makes writing for anthropology different from the kinds of writing you may be used to doing for other courses. Here are six expectations to keep in mind.

### Critical Distance

Thinking like an anthropologist means not only doing fieldwork but also having a healthy skepticism about the world. Achieving *critical distance* means stepping back enough from your own perspective to do relatively dispassionate interpretation and analysis.

In another sense, valuing critical distance means having the courage to speak up. As anthropologists do their fieldwork and perform analyses, they often arrive at conclusions that other people feel threatened by. In "When Social Science is Doing Its Job," Thomas J. Pettigrew [13] explains:

> Pointing out social dilemmas and unintended consequences usually means providing negative feedback about society.

It means adopting a critical stance about the society to which social scientists themselves belong. As messengers of bad tidings, social scientists find this an unpopular role to play. It sometimes requires the courage of a resident of 17th-century Salem, Massachusetts who publicly doubted the reality of witches. Some people even regard such criticism of the nation as "un-American." Negative feedback remains a professional duty of social scientists, however, even if the advice is ignored and the scientist is abused.

Working as an anthropologist requires having the inquisitiveness to ask the difficult questions and the bravery to communicate them to others. As a student you might not want to take on big challenges, but you will find that thinking "against the grain" and pursuing ideas—even when they are unfamiliar, uncomfortable, and unpopular—will be rewarding. Even simply sharing your own interpretation of a text when the majority of the class is pulling in a different direction can signal a healthy critical distance. Keep this in mind when it comes to writing.

## Engagement

One of key words for anthropology at the moment is *engagement*. That term may seem almost the opposite of *distance*, but especially for cultural anthropologists, participating in a culture or community is an essential method for understanding and analyzing it.

If you look over the syllabi of anthropology courses, you may notice similarities in course goals:

... challenge previous conceptions about ...
... think about global and local contexts ...
... use a variety of perspectives to evaluate information ...
... develop a better understanding of humanity ...

... engage in scholarly research ...
... discuss how culture influences thinking and
behavior ...

Engagement may not appear on each syllabus, but you are in
fact *invited* to engage with the habits of mind, critical methods,
and ongoing conversations in the field. In this book, I use the
term *engagement* both in this sense and in the much broader
intellectual sense of naming meaningful interactions that
result in enhanced understandings for an anthropologist (or
student of anthropology). Therefore, using research to take
a position on an issue is engagement. Actively and critically
interpreting art, film, or fieldnotes constitutes engagement.
Asking your own questions and identifying methods to
answer them is engagement.

## Reflexivity

Reflexivity is a process of self-reference and the "ways in which
the products of research are affected by the personnel and
process of doing research" [14]. The concept of reflexivity developed during the 1960s and 1970s [15] and has become more
important in recent decades. Reflexivity was a "correction" to
a previous format of ethnographic writing "in which factual
material was presented by an omniscient yet invisible author-
narrator whose methods of fieldwork and data collecting were
not always manifest, and who did not address the effect of her
or his presence on others, much less the various effects that
others may have had on her or him" [16].

Today, there are many different ways to express reflexive
writing. Wanda Pillow [17] identified four common trends in
present-day uses of reflexivity: (1) reflexivity as recognition of
self; (2) reflexivity as recognition of other; (3) reflexivity as
truth; and (4) reflexivity as transcendence. Reflexivity should
inform how anthropologists—and students of anthropology—
approach their methods and communicate their findings [18].

The American Anthropological Association associates *engaged anthropology* more specifically with activism: "An engaged anthropology is committed to supporting social change efforts that arise from the interaction between community goals and anthropological research." Beck and Maida [1] offer a fuller endorsement for using the tools of anthropology to pursue social justice:

> While anthropologists continue to act as decoders of cultures that are different and look difficult to understand or appreciate by society at large, it is critical for us to become more instrumental. We must participate in generating and bringing about change. We must be engaged in protecting the most vulnerable from oppression and exploitation and support the empowerment of communities to improve people's lives. This is a role not comfortably taken by tradition-bound anthropologists; however, an engaged stance moves the application of anthropological theory, methods and practice further along towards action and activism. At the same time, engagement moves anthropologists away from traditional forms of participant observation towards a participatory role by becoming increasingly a part of those communities or social groupings that we normally study.

*Engagement* features in the title of books like *Toward Engaged Anthropology* by Beck and Maida [1], a range of articles [4], and even funding sources such as the Engaged Anthropology Grant. There's even a blog called "Engagement" that works at the intersections of anthropology and environmental problems.

## Cultural Relativism

Cultural relativism is the concept that human beliefs and behaviors should be understood by the standards of that culture, not by the culture of the analyst. Members of the public might say "primitive" but anthropologists are alert to the complicated colonial connotations embedded in this word, especially since anthropologists themselves previously used it. We anthropologists do not call the people we work with "subjects" because that term can dehumanize them. Anthropologists likewise are hypersensitive to ethnocentrism, which is the evaluation of other people by one's own cultural standards. For example, the following sentence violates the principle of cultural relativism: "One can easily figure out just how wasteful our culture is, even with a higher intellect than many other cultures." This statement is ethnocentric because the writer assumes that his culture has a "higher intellect" than people of other cultures, and it is not clear exactly who the "we" is that he's referring to. Students tend to use the pronouns "we" and "our" to refer to their own cultural background without considering the possibility that their reader might not share that background. Other words that cause concern are words such as "weird," "normal," and "traditional" because those words indicate a judgment or indictment. By whose standards is a behavior normal? Whose traditions are we really talking about?

Anthropologists tend to emphasize cultural relativism very early in introductory classes because we want students to understand that they may encounter things in their lives that contradict their worldviews. We are quick to react to essentialism, which is the belief that a culture or a people is composed of a set of unchanging, fixed traits. This is "one of the besetting conceptual sins in anthropology" [19] because "the position that once one is a human being one has a certain set of characteristics is unpopular, especially among social scientists who often argue in favour of a cultural, socially, and individually constructed human identity" (Brezina 2013, 78). Cultural relativism, ethnocentrism, and essentialism may seem like abstract philosophical concepts, but the more you are aware them, the more deliberate you will be in your work choices—and the less often you will lapse into common phrasings that irk anthropologists.

## Context/History

Anthropologists value long memories and see time, like culture, as relative: 2,000 years ago, for example, is not that long if you are looking at the earliest evidence of *Homo sapiens*, which dates to 200,000 years ago [21]. Likewise, writing that an event happened "long ago" simply is not precise enough for anthropology. Good anthropologists identify and explain smaller details as part of broader patterns.

Showing history requires doing the appropriate background research. All anthropology is *contextualized*; in other words, you should put your specific research question in some broader context to connect your question to other related timelines, ideas, and research questions. For example, the sentence, "Ritual behaviors occur in many contexts" will not work without being followed by elaboration of the contexts where and when specific ritualized behaviors have occurred.

## Description

Professors in some fields will warn you away from including too much description in your academic writing because they see it as filler or as a poor substitute for analysis. Yet anthropologists see description as an essential partner to analysis. Indeed, most anthropological writing involves an attempt to describe some human problem. If it happens in the past, the goal is to reconstruct life and behavior based on the specimens, fossils, and artifacts that remain. If it is a current human

| Thin Description | Diagnosis | Better/Thicker Description |
|---|---|---|
| "Someone studying my garbage will be able to identify different aspects of my life." | Provide some examples. What criteria would archaeologists use to study the materials in trash? How would they determine what the objects' original purposes were? What are the found objects made of? How could the objects be matched to aspects of your life? | "Someone studying my garbage will be able to identify different aspects of my life. With enough garbage, I am sure that some patterns would emerge, such as coffee grinds and wrappers of my favorite junk food. Some objects that I frequently use every day, such as my computer, wouldn't end up in the garbage because it is a more durable product than food and because of how it should be properly disposed. An archaeologist wouldn't get a completely accurate picture of my daily life by looking only at my trash." |
| "The interview was brief." | Too vague. What counts as "brief"? What happened before, during, or after the interview that suggests that the interview took very little time to complete? | "The interview lasted only 10 minutes because the interviewee arrived late and said that he had to leave early. The other interviews lasted about 30 minutes, so this interview took only a third of the time. The interviewee provided yes or no questions to eight out of the ten questions asked. He frequently looked at his watch and elaborated further only when the interviewer asked him a follow-up question." |

problem such as health disparities in New York City, the goal is to depict the lived experience.

If you are using original data, how do you do justice to what people told you in interviews or surveys? How do you present this data? Geertz [22] would want you to stick to "thick description," which calls for sharing specific stories and including telling details—for *showing* rather than just *telling*. In practical terms, this means that your anthropology papers may contain more textured description than do papers for many of your other classes (although description *alone* will not cut it, nor will gratuitously long descriptions untethered from a guiding purpose). The degree of description in this student sample below might be excessive in some other courses, but in anthropology the "Better/Thicker Description" version is the norm.

As you develop as a writer in anthropology, you will grow more and more comfortable with the field expectations for these six core values and practices. You will also find yourself cumulatively adding more concerns, such as structure, conflict, power, inequality, and agency.

# WRITING CRITIQUES, RESPONSE PAPERS, AND BOOK/FILM REVIEWS

Write as if you mean it, and write as if what you write can change the reader. Because it will.
—William Germano, Dean of Humanities at Cooper Union, in Brooks and Jewett (2014, 101)

If you have ever posted a review of a restaurant, hotel, or book on a website, or taken a survey assessing someone's performance, you have already participated in a review: You have interpreted and judged another person's effort. These days, online reviews abound, and they have a real effect on readers' opinions. But think back to the reviews that you have given more weight. They were not the quick scores or rants ("I hated my hotel room") but instead those that matched telling evidence to claims ("The king-size bed was actually two double beds pushed together"). It is important to be critical, but it is also important to support the critique with evidence.

This chapter provides strategies for critiques (including compare/contrast papers), response papers, and book/film reviews. These assignments are critical in orientation and narrative in structure. They are shorter than literature reviews and research papers and are often used as warmups or skill-building exercises in anticipation of those longer projects. Critiques,

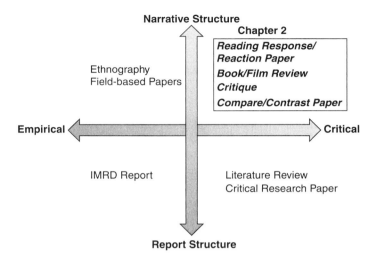

FIGURE 2.1 Structure and Approach for Critiques, Response Papers, and Book/Film Reviews.

response papers, and reviews can even be used to test out ideas that you might want to develop later in a more formal assignment.

These assignments get you to evaluate, analyze, compare/contrast, explain, and interpret secondary information so that you can come to your own conclusions about it—all essential intellectual habits. For any of these papers, you might have page or word limits, so seek guidance from your instructor in addition to the advice presented in this chapter.

## Critiques

The critique is an exercise in critical thinking in which you evaluate the strengths and weaknesses of a source. Instead of readily accepting what the author writes, you are charged with evaluating the ideas the author has presented. This challenge can be daunting, especially if you are a newcomer to the field.

Here are some suggestions for writing a good critique paper:

- *Summarize* the original text, article, or book, identifying *both* the author's *main ideas* and *purpose*. The trick here is to be brief; if more than half of the paper (or half of any page of your paper) is summary, that's probably too much.
- *Divide* the argument into smaller elements that can be more readily critiqued, such as underlying assumptions, methods, hypotheses, evidence, modes of argument, or conclusions
- *Identify* the logic behind those smaller elements—although usually just one element or a subset of them. One strategy here is to show readers that you understand the full scope of possibilities but have chosen to focus on one or a few. For example, "While I understand that Jones is doing X, Y, and Z, I will focus my critique on his methods [or his underlying assumptions, or his interpretation of evidence, or the conclusions he draws, or . . .] because . . ."
- *Explain* how each major element relates to and builds upon the previous element (or explains how each element should relate and doesn't build upon the previous element), if you are charged with doing a more comprehensive review
- *Conclude* by *exploring the implications* of your critique.

Writing a good critique means that you have a handle on the original text so that you can summarize it, analyze it (reduce it to its parts and see what you have), and then evaluate how well the parts fit together when you try to reconstruct them on your own. What assumptions is the author relying on? What assumptions does the theory rely on? Are there any faulty assumptions or flaws in logic?

Here's an example of a brief critique written by a first-year graduate student:

Marvin Harris (1992) uses historical explanations and empirical generalization to
argue that the source of cow worship in
India is a result of ecology instead of Hindu
theology in his article "The Cultural Ecology of India's Sacred Cattle." In order to
use these explanations, he makes several
assumptions. First, he assumes that he
can analyze the situation without ever
having been to India and bases his arguments upon preexisting literature (51).
Harris also assumes that human beings
will make choices that improve their lives.
He argues that "much more likely the relationship between bovines and humans is
symbiotic instead of competitive. It probably represents the outcome of intense
Darwinian pressures acting upon human
and bovine population" (52). In the Indian
society, the cow fills this role as a useful
animal.

⟵ First paragraph intro-
duces the research and
the author, assump-
tions, and main
arguments.

Harris uses a historical explanation when
he describes how a food crisis during
World War II caused an increase in cattle
slaughter and threatened the doctrine of
*ahimsa* (57). This trend led to anti-slaughter
legislation. Harris's use of historical explanation strengthens his empirical generalization because it describes a particular
timeline when changes in ecology, not religious belief, challenged *ahimsa*.

⟵ Second paragraph de-
scribes the explanation
the author uses and
what kind of explanation
it is.

These assumptions form the basis for the
empirical generalization that the sacred-
ness of cattle stems from their usefulness
in that particular ecology rather than religious belief. Harris writes that the "degree
of observance of taboos against bovine

⟵ Third paragraph
rebuilds the pieces—
the assumption and
explanation—into an
evaluation of how well
the author arrived at a
hypothesis.

slaughter and beef-eating reflect the power
of these ecological pressures rather than
*ahimsa*; in other words, *ahimsa* itself derives
power and sustenance from the material
rewards it confers upon both men and animals" (52). In an empirical generalization,
the dependent variable is a function of an
independent variable, and Harris states that
the cattle worship occurs as a result of
ecology. Harris' use of empirical generalization works well in this article because not
only does it clearly assign variables to
answer the question of why cattle worship
exists in India but it also creates a testable
hypothesis.

The **compare/contrast paper** is a critique of two or more
sources. The compare/contrast format is commonly used in
take-home exams that require writing essay responses. The
assignment asks you to do everything that you would do for
a critique paper, but here you have two sources. If you are
writing a compare/contrast paper in which you are comparing two theories or research articles, use the following
process.

## Draw Up a "Fact Sheet"

Use one half of the paper to lay out the building blocks of the
article: the assumptions, theories, methods, findings, and conclusions of one article down the page. Use the other half of the
paper to outline the building blocks of the second article. This
way, you stay organized and can make meaningful comparisons
when you write the paper. If your assignment asks you to identify the more scientifically sound article, be sure to state this
early as a thesis statement and restate at the end of the paper
where you explain how your major points brought you to that
conclusion.

## Organize Your Draft According to Readers' Expectations

In your introduction, briefly summarize each paper. Then make your thesis statement. Your thesis statement should *not* be "There are similarities and differences" or "There are many significant similarities and differences between these two articles." We know! That was the whole point of the assignment. Instead, consider:

- Is there something *about* the similarities (or the differences) that you can point to that would be the frame for your paper?
- Relative strengths and weaknesses?
- Comparison of the positions being presented by the authors?

If the assignment asks you to state explicitly which of the two works is the better, more superior research, then your answer to this question is your thesis statement.

## Follow the Compare/Contrast Logic Through the Paper

To write up the comparison, you have two options:

- Show all the similarities and then follow with all the differences (for example, S1, S2, S3, S4, D1, D2, D3, D4). If you have two research articles, for example, you could compare, section by section, the approach, methods, findings, and implications of the research conducted.
- Show the similarity and differences for each point (for example, S1, D1, S2, D2, S3, D3, S4, D4). Point-by-point style is more difficult to achieve. Why? Each point would need two similar things for the comparison to work, and finding these kind of similarities is not always possible.

## Conclude with Implications

The real intellectual action of such a paper, however, is never in simply taking an inventory of similarities or differences but in pursuing the implications of those similarities and differences. This is the "so what?" factor that is so important in anthropological writing and must be in the conclusion section.

# Response Papers

Reading responses are cousins to critiques. You are still identifying the author's main arguments and including your opinions on those arguments, supported by examples from the text, but reading responses give you a bit more flexibility to personalize your narrative.

At the surface level, instructors want to know you are doing the reading, but more importantly, they want to know what you can bring to the conversation as a critical thinker. To quote writing studies scholar Joseph Harris (2006, 36), academic writing "does not reply to the texts it cites so much as *forwards* passages and ideas from them." You are not trying to come to a definite answer that will shut down the ongoing debate; instead, you are entering the multitude of ideas and introducing your own. Move the conversation forward.

What does a reading response look like? For some classes, the response is a 100-word blog post. For others it is a three-page paper with an introduction, thesis statement, and conclusion.

The best responses:

- must be more than summaries
- show a genuine connection to the reading, even if that connection is negative
- are never purely personal
- demonstrate what *about* the reading interested you, how you interpreted the reading, how you applied abstract

concepts from the reading, and what connections you can make within or across readings.

In the end, your instructor wants to see honesty, well-thought-out ideas, and evidence that you have done some analytical legwork.

When writing a response paper, try the following process:

## Consider Your Response to the Text

Reaction papers are, in part, about attitude. To get you started, think about the overall tone of the text and some reactions to what you read. Here are three possible directions:

- Your emotion or state of mind as you read the text
- The *tone* of the author's writing
- The quality of the text itself.

*Tone* is the perspective that the author has toward the subject matter, the audience or characters he or she is writing about. Students in introductory courses might read a variety of writings collected in an anthology, so they come in contact with different writers, different writing styles, different subject matter, and so forth. Not all authors will approach writing exactly the same way, and how they approach their writing is made up of deliberate decisions that you, the reader, should identify. The third possible direction is to evaluate the quality of the writing itself, using the standards of clear writing.

1. Your emotion. Here are some examples of emotional reaction words that students use in reading responses:

| Positive | Negative |
|----------|----------|
| amazed | anxious |
| intrigued | frustrated |
| certain | upset |

|           |              |
|-----------|--------------|
| curious   | disappointed |
| motivated | concerned    |

2. Author's tone. The following "tone words" are presented without being ordered into "positive" and "negative" because the interpretation is based on the reader's point of view. Under most circumstances, anthropologists use a serious tone for their audiences, but this is not always the case. Here are some "tone words" that students can use in writing reading responses:

|               |          |
|---------------|----------|
| critical      | serious  |
| light-hearted | informal |
| optimistic    | angry    |
| sad           | dramatic |
| witty         | pompous  |

3. Quality of the text. Here are some reaction words relating to the quality of the text that can be used by students writing reading responses:

| Positive   | Negative      |
|------------|---------------|
| clear      | difficult     |
| current    | outdated      |
| satisfying | dissatisfying |
| engrossing | boring        |
| thoughtful | ambivalent    |

Reaction words require you to provide further explanation because they are "pointing words" that signal to a reader, "OK, what should come immediately afterward is elaboration on what caused this particular reaction." It is not enough to write, "The sequence of events that the author described made me nervous." Your reader will stop reading your paper and think, "Wait—which events made you nervous? Would they make me nervous, too? Not knowing which events made you nervous is now making *me* nervous ..."

## Start Your Response with a Focus

Rather than trying to connect your response to a universal problem, stick closely to the reading. For example, you might start your paper:

- With a direct quotation from the text
- With a provocative statement that turns on a tension: "While many think X, I think the author is instead ..."
- With a question at the beginning and/or throughout. "After finishing the article on arranged marriage, I asked myself, 'Do I know anyone whose marriage was arranged?'"

For such a brief, introspective assignment, the introduction has two purposes: (1) summarize the original work and (2) summarize your argument/analysis/reflection. Your instructor will want evidence that you have read or viewed carefully, so some summary is necessary. When some students try to do this, however, they end up trying to cover everything. Instead, you should highlight specific points to focus on. As a general rule, devote three or four sentences of the first paragraph of the response paper to your summary.

Most response papers should include at least one direct quotation, either to introduce what you will focus on or to support claims you make.

## Use Analysis to Guide Your Response

Some typical moves for your analysis are as follows:

- Trace a theme in the text (but not a theme that is so obvious as to not need tracing) and show how it develops.

- Focus on and unpack one key term.
- Question the author about something that is vague, debatable, ambiguous, or dubious in the text.
- Show how different elements of the work relate to one another (after all, the etymology of *analysis* is "to break down into parts" or "to dissolve").
- Point out an inconsistency between different elements of the text or a paradox.
- Raise a question the author did not raise.
- Apply the author's claim to a new context.
- Identify and unpack some underlying, unstated assumptions the writer makes: "When Claire Sterk (2000) uses the religious term 'fallen women' in her book to describe women who engage in prostitution, this is not her opinion but the opinions of the social workers, police, pimps and customers who believe they have fallen from grace for doing something morally wrong."
- Connect the reading to a reading or concept from another course. Warning: Do this only if you can make a *clear* connection between the two readings or courses. You do not want to make it look like you are having difficulty engaging with the assigned reading—or worse, like you are reusing an old paper for a current class.

## Connect Your Reaction to the Analysis

There are several rhetorical strategies you can use to connect your reaction to the analysis, including the following:

- Connect the text to something you have experienced in your own life: "The author's description of exogamy reminded me of my own family . . ."
- Recognize an emotional reaction you are having to the text and respond to it: "I was frustrated by the way the writer omitted . . ."

- Connect the text to something you have been discussing in class: "Gmelch's use of the term 'magic' in 'Baseball Magic' relates to our class discussions about superstitions . . ."

Remember, your job is not to prove you did the reading by summarizing or saying something that is incontrovertibly true. Instead, your job is to *open up* and *stoke* the conversation. As the epigraph to this chapter suggests, your job is to be provocative, to change the thinking of your readers, or at least to help them see new connections.

Here are the last two paragraphs of a first draft of a response paper to the story "Eating Christmas in the Kalahari" by Richard Lee (2007):

The article becomes less formal and had the style of a story. It had a plot, a setting, "characters"; all the elements of a story. The lesson that Lee learns at the end is mirrored by morality present in story-telling, which had a huge impact for me when I read it. It was as if the plot of the story paralleled the style of the article. Lee learned that the !Kung Bushmen demolished any sign of pride and arrogance by insulting every kill everyone made: "Yes, when a young man kills much meat he comes to think of himself as a chief or a big man, and he thinks of the rest of us as his servants or inferiors. We can't accept this" (21). It kept a sense of balance and unity within the tribe. Lee found out about this custom first hand as he was continually insulted for buying an ox that was characterized as a "bag of bones." He could not figure out how his ox was so unappetizing and it upset him very much. At the end of the story that he found out that it was the custom of the tribe. Lee's displayed knowledge in the beginning of the article made no mention of this. What I got from the story is that even

← Good move: The student identifies the anthropologist's writing style as a narrative where the author is also the main character. The student also explains how a narrative style affects her as the reader.

← Good move: The student weaves summary with quotes to illustrate her points.

experts still have something to learn and the way it was written emphasized that.

If Lee had not written the article as a story, but as a repetition of facts like in the beginning of the article, I do not think it would have been as interesting. I was really interested because I wanted to know what was wrong with the ox. I got a lot out of it, which is sort of the point.

← Bad move: The student ends the final sentence in a wishy-washy way instead of writing in a more decisive way. The last phrase "which is sort of the point" is unnecessary.

Mediocre move: The student repeats "interesting/interested" in two adjoining sentences. "Interesting" is an empty phrase without explanation.

## Book/Film Reviews

Reviewing the work of others is a regular practice for professional anthropologists, who review books, articles, films, and even exhibits. Reviewing gives professionals a chance to see the most current work of others, identify new directions of the field, and assess each other's research. In your class, you might be asked to find a peer-reviewed article in a scholarly journal and write a review. Some professional anthropologists might be asked to review several books or films together, which requires the anthropologist to unite everything under a theme.

Reviews also appear as regular sections of subject-specific journals either with a unique title or the name of the work being reviewed. If you are looking for models, two places to read professionals reviewing professionals are the review sections of *American Anthropologist* or the Anthropology Review Database.

The book/film review is an exercise in information extraction, as you'll need to distill many pages or minutes into usually around 1,000 words for a review. For the book/film review paper, you should give recommendations for what audience is best suited for the book or film.

The best book/film reviews have the following characteristics:

- They summarize briefly the author's main arguments. The summary should never make up the majority of the review.
- They put the book or film in context: its history, its intended audience, its significance related to similar works, etc.
- They evaluate the strengths and weaknesses of the book or film.
- They identify underlying assumptions, distinctive features, implications, or something otherwise interesting about the work.

## What's the Difference Between a Book/Film Review, Critique, and Response Paper?

The book/film review is more personal than a critique and gives you more opportunities to write "I," but it is actually less personal than the response paper. In a response paper, the writer attempts to walk the reader through the text alongside the writer as if they are in a garden together, pointing out certain details and describing what inspired the writer and why. To use the same garden analogy, the writer of a book or film review is simply looking at the garden as a whole first, trying to assess what purpose the garden is serving and how well the gardener met that purpose. Then, the writer looks at specific details to explain why the gardener succeeded or did not. The aspect of "successful/not successful" also appears in the response, because many of the feelings a text might provoke come from how well the writer made his or her own point. In a book or film review, the item being reviewed is being measured against the professional standards for anthropology.

When writing a book/film review, try the following process:

## Craft a Vivid Introduction

The following is from a review by Miriam Lee Kaprow (1985) of the book *Risk and Culture: An Essay on the Selection of Technological and Environmental Dangers* by Mary Douglas and Aaron Wildavsky. The first vivid sentences grab the reader's attention:

We live in a world encompassed by fear. Americans, say Douglas and Wildavsky, are afraid of "Nothing much . . . except the food they eat, the water they drink, the air they breathe, the land they live on, and the energy they use" (p. 10). This fear, they correctly point out, has accelerated over the past 15 to 20 years, even as health in the United States and other industrialized countries has continued to improve. Moreover, they add, we often choose our terrors and nightmares, for each society selects just a few dangers and ignores a vast range of others.

← The book that Kaprow is reviewing is about fear and risk, so maybe it is easier for her to shock the reader than someone with a more mundane topic, but what she is doing is pointing out that all societies have a sense of fear but what people fear is not always the same. She singles out Americans because the authors did in the book—the humorous quote provides a convenient way in to the review.

It helps the reader if you create mental pictures with your words—remember, your audience is reading your review, not the original text. Through just one word, "correctly," you know that Kaprow is in agreement with the authors—and you know she's an American because she uses "we" in the last sentence.

Here's an excerpt of a student's review of an *Anthropology Today* article:

Although many anthropologists and sociologists "applied their skills in support of the First World War, it was the Second World War that brought the widespread application of anthropology to the practice of warfare" (Price, 2001). A large majority of anthropologists joined the war effort out of a sense of patriotism and realization of the Nazis' threat to humanity. Many anthropologists applied their skills to areas such as domestic propaganda, policy analysis, and covert missions in which they used their credentials as a cover for clandestine operations (Price, 2001). Other anthropologists, however, began to voice their concerns about the use of anthropological methods for warfare and the subsequent betrayal of the cultures they studied. Price uses this historical analysis to raise further ethical questions about the military's current application of anthropology in the "War on Terror."

*← Good move: The student starts with a quote, similar to the technique used by Kaprow. Then he summarizes the article, identifies the major differences between anthropologists on the issue, as described by the author, and summarizes the merits of the work.*

This article presents valuable information about the degree to which anthropologists were involved with U.S. intelligence and war agencies during the Second World War. It explains some of the anthropologists' motivations for assuming different roles and tasks during the war. It also presents the positive and negative consequences of their actions. Similar to "Anthropologists as Spies," this article provides a historical perspective of the relationship between anthropology and the military/intelligence communities.

## Evaluate the Work

Identify the strengths and weaknesses of the book/film, using quotations to illustrate your points. Most students worry that they will sound too negative in their review, but only rarely does a reviewer state that someone's work has no redeeming qualities, so you can include some elements of praise. Conversely, even if you like a work, you can still point out some shortcomings:

The quality of this excellent book is not diminished by identifying a few points in which
the discussion could be further elaborated or
where, in the opinion of this reviewer at least,
Ashforth's judgment is questionable. For
example, in considering what governments
might do about witchcraft fears and witchcraft accusations, Ashforth has missed a
broader literature, particularly on West
Africa, that could have been useful. Similarly,
he may be unduly pessimistic in his assessment of the chances of registering healers
and of including traditional religion in school
curricula, as a closer look at Zimbabwe and
Zambia might have indicated. And, although
Ashforth is to be congratulated on including
in his bibliography some of the most salient
literature by South African theologians, his
analysis of the possible role of churches in
providing a greater sense of spiritual security is rather perfunctory (Ellis 2006).

Style note: "In the opin-
ion of this reviewer"
removes the need for an
"I" statement but is
more wordy. Feel free
to use "I" statements in
your review; if you really
want to use "this re-
viewer" once or twice
for variety, that's OK,
but the simpler (and
less pretentious) "I"
tends to be the better
move.

In addition to pointing out the strengths and weaknesses
of the book or film, you can also use the following strategies:

- Analyze just one key scene. Don't forget to explain what
  makes the scene "key," and include as many details from
  the scene in your analysis.
- Think about issues of power: How does the filmmaker deal
  with the already-unequal power relationship between the
  researcher and the people being filmed? Whose point of
  view is privileged? Are you, as the audience, being shielded
  from some of the reality being presented, through camera
  angles? What decisions is the director making that create
  some distance between the audience and the subject matter,
  and are these decisions appropriate?

- Listen to the narrator. If there's a narrator, is he or she omniscient? Is the narrator necessary or noticeable (in a bad way)? What's the tone of the narrator compared to the action going on in the film? Does the narrator speak more like a researcher or like the group being studied?
- Take a concept or key term introduced earlier in the semester and apply it to the film.
- Examine what choices the filmmaker makes. For example, does the editing of two shots or scenes purposely create an emotional or associative response in the viewer? How do those choices parallel specific anthropological concepts? Do any film choices conflict with anthropological concepts?
- If you are very stuck, look at the metadata about the film online. Who funded the film? What was the distribution of the film? External information about the film might give you insight into potential biases displayed in the film.
- Bring in outside sources. Are there published reviews that you can introduce into your paper to compare/contrast with your own ideas? (Check a database like Anthrosource.)
- Who or what interests benefit from the making and distribution of this film?

## A Final Word on Reviewing Ethnographic Films

The history of ethnographic film is as old as visual recording technology itself (De Brigard 2003). Ethnographic films are produced by filmmakers concerned with culture and were originally used to document "primitive" people and colonialism. Today's filmmakers are concerned about what counts as ethnographic film, the similarities and differences between ethnography and film, and the extent to which filmmakers generate truth through film (Heider 2007). Therefore, film is an important medium for understanding humanity. In fact, as Karl Heider (2007, 9) argues, "An ethnographic film can only be as good as the understanding that precedes the filmmaking." You may be asked to review an ethnographic film. Use the techniques already presented in this chapter, but also pay attention to:

| | |
|---|---|
| "Staged" behaviors | Point of view |
| Camera angles | Shots of full bodies |
| Editing | Sound (ambient noises) |
| Ethnographer's presence in the film | Sound (musical score or soundtrack) |
| Fictional recreations | Subjects speaking to the camera |
| Narration | Subtitles |

For all of the assignments discussed in this chapter, do not just summarize the text; use the text as a launching pad for your own interpretations, ideas, and arguments. And do not end your paper with a summary of what you just said—remember, these are short papers and readers do not need a summary at both ends. Instead, raise questions, or discuss the potential implications of what you have proposed or how readers might continue pursuing the line of inquiry you have started.

## Ask yourself:

Does the film convey core anthropological values? Which ones? To what extent does the film successfully convey them?

What makes the film seem authentic? Inauthentic?

What was the director's intent? How do you know? Does that intent match the finished product? Why or why not?

# NAVIGATING FIELD-BASED ASSIGNMENTS

> Fieldwork itself is humanly demanding, as a fieldworker
> will need to give proof of all the good qualities in life:
> patience, endurance, stamina, perseverance, flexibility,
> adaptability, empathy, tolerance, the willingness to lose a
> battle to win a war, creativity, humour and wit, diplomacy,
> and being happy about small achievements. Put that in a
> job advertisement and you will never find a suitable
> candidate.
>
> —Jan Blommaert and Dong Jie (2010, 24)

> I have notes! And quotes! Now what do I do?
> —One of my students new to ethnographic research

Ah, the field. You might have noticed your anthropology instructor get a wistful, faraway look when he or she starts to talk
about fieldwork. In Brazil, they call that feeling *saudade*, an
overwhelming sense of nostalgia. Fieldwork is often romanticized and exoticized. Fieldwork can be thrilling—infinitely
better and more memorable than any vacation, because fieldworkers are not tourists. They are the "professional strangers" (Agar 1980) who enter a site, someone else's space, and

*somehow* begin to build rapport with the people around them. They gain a foothold in a new culture/environment/society and eventually gain enough trust to enter people's homes, make friends, and conduct in-depth interviews. That "somehow" in the previous sentence is the ethnographic "toolkit" (Schensul and LeCompte 1999). Of course, you do not need to go far from home to do this work.

Yet, fieldwork is unpredictable. It is important that anthropology students accept this fact as early as possible in their careers, even as they do their best to adhere to the practical strategies that have guided past fieldworkers and ethical best practices. Apart from experiencing logistical catastrophes such as bad weather and missed flights, anthropologists can run out of funding, have permissions that were previously granted revoked, or encounter all variety of obstacles. Some days in the field are so stressful that it feels like you are being tested by the anthropology gods. Others are quite boring. But fieldwork is important, often likened to a rite of passage for the new professional anthropologist.

Some anthropologists are only truly happy when in the field, because everything happens in real time, creating a full, 360-degree experience. But students who are new to fieldwork call it "awkward" or "anxiety-provoking"—because it certainly can be. Anthropologist Mike Agar (1980, 83) reflects on how stepping out of the relative comforts of traditional academic work and into the field can trigger self-consciousness, even fear:

> You arrive, tape recorder in hand, with a grin rigidly planted on your face. You probably realise that you have no idea how your grin is being interpreted, so you stop and nervously attempt a relaxed pose. Then you realise you have no idea how that is being interpreted. Soon you work

yourself into the paralysis of the psychiatrist in the strip joint—she knows she can't react, but she knows she can't not react. It is little wonder that sometimes people hide in a hotel room and read mysteries.

I had a student once who asked for permission to take a Xanax® before she did her assignment. She was joking, but fieldwork is likely to make you feel vulnerable because it takes you outside the comfort zone of typical academic work. You are working in plain sight, so you are visible, and especially if you are conducting an observation, you might feel like you are *spying* on people's behaviors as they conduct their daily activities. Always remember that your

## Top Ways Students Tend to Misunderstand Field-Based Assignments

1. Thinking they are being graded on a scale of "right" versus "wrong" instead of "does the account provide enough detail for a reader to have a picture of what happened, with an analysis of the behaviors observed?"
2. Treating their observations as fact instead of as open to interpretation
3. Forgetting all about reflexivity—they do not consider how aspects of their identity, such as their social class, gender, or race, might affect their perceptions or how others perceive them
4. Omitting the seemingly mundane—but in fact quite important—"who, what, where, when" descriptions of the setting early in the report.

participants and the community where you conduct your research are stakeholders in the research. Fieldwork has ramifications for the researcher as well as the research "subjects," as the Institutional Review Board (IRB) describes human participants. You cannot conduct fieldwork without permissions in place, and you cannot conduct research without an ethics review. For classroom assignments, instructors secure IRB approvals, but students interested in conducting their own research should familiarize themselves with their institution's IRB.

But how do you get from fieldwork observations to written products such as articles and books? Through stories. Fieldwork stories, as George E. Marcus (2009, 19) writes in the introduction to *Fieldwork Is Not What it Used to Be*, "are the medium by which anthropologists reveal to one another what really goes on in fieldwork." The classical written product of social and cultural anthropologists is *ethnography*, the scientific description of the customs of individual peoples and cultures; this word's roots are "people" or "culture" and "writing."

This chapter demystifies field-based work such as observation or participant-observation assignments, writing basic fieldnotes, and conducting mini-ethnographies. When students embrace field exercises and apply the kinds of principles discussed in this chapter, they can return from doing fieldwork with detailed, relevant, observation-driven stories to share. If you look at our familiar diagram of genres in anthropology, you will see that ethnography and other ethnographic, field-based assignments are different from the other genres in this book.

Ethnography is empirical because it requires firsthand original data collection, but the structure of the written work is narrative. Take, for example, an assignment that required students to observe a section of a grocery store. One student conscientiously chose to observe the bread aisle in a superstore because he considered bread a "vital food product." He had several findings. First, he noticed that people keep their distance from each other while in the aisle. The extra-wide aisles in a superstore probably facilitate this phenomenon. Second, he was surprised to find tortillas in the aisle because, as he later reflected, "I do not consider tortillas bread." Finally, he observed that people multitask while shopping—he saw a woman argue with her child while she searched for her bread. For students, these assignments develop new ways of seeing the world.

"Fieldwork is two things.

"First, it is the ethnographer acting as a research instrument. Just like a survey questionnaire, or a focus-group video camera, the ethnographer herself collects all the data.

"Second, fieldwork is the symbolic act of 'walking in the shoes' of your participants. By physically going to another location, the ethnographer is leaving behind that which she knows and, in some cases, controls. She is becoming a member of her participants' world and choosing willfully to follow their rules and adopt their ways. This is the critical step of establishing rapport. Rapport underpins qualitative research generally, but ethnography in particular. These twin activities are what differentiates ethnographic fieldwork from other research experiences and it is what is so cognitively and emotionally draining about ethnography." (Ladner 2014, 117)

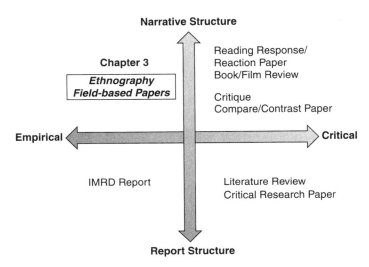

FIGURE 3.1  Structure and Approach for Field-Based Assignments.

## Understanding the Assignment

Professors assign fieldwork to help students become familiar with professional methods. A secondary motive is often to "decenter" the student, which is part of becoming a reflective and ethical practitioner.

Field-based assignments can include mapping terrain, photographing your daily environment, interviewing someone, observing an event, or recording behavior at a venue such as a workplace, restaurant, museum, or sporting event. All such assignments have the same underlying expectation: that you will hone your perceptive skills by writing descriptively about what you are observing. Such assignments demand not only notetaking but also interpretation.

Field-based assignments may seem simple—just get out there, observe, and take notes—but they are in fact quite

**Biggest Mistakes Students Make While
Completing a Field-Based Assignment**

1. Having a false sense of security that this kind of assignment is something anyone can do
2. Worrying about the worst-case scenario and becoming paralyzed in the field
3. Assuming that using electronics ensures a better field experience
4. Having difficulty deciding what to focus on.

complex, and should not be underestimated. Usually, students write either too few or too many notes and then are overwhelmed about how to start their analysis and write-up. You *must* have a research question, even for short assignments. While preliminary fieldwork may be needed to help define or refine the research question, the question should be identified before systematic data collection begins.

## Managing the Data

Before collecting data, consider how you will manage that data:

- How will you organize, store, or retrieve data?
- How will you keep participants' personal information safe?
- If it is a quantitative survey, what will the database look like?
- What software will you use? Do you even need software for your project?
- What will the variables be named?
- How will you organize them?

- If you are using qualitative one-on-one interviews, how will you keep them once they've been transcribed into text?
- What will you call the filenames?
- How will you store photos and fieldnotes?

Answering such questions will help you formulate a strategy and select a technology for organizing the data you collect.

Keep this in mind: Some anthropologists believe that you should not use technologies—except a pencil or pen—to collect and analyze your data. These professors worry that you are letting the technology do the work that you should be doing with your brain. Whether you're using a program that analyzes data for you or one that merely facilitates key steps in research, your job is to use your brain to interpret that data earnestly and transform it into information. When in doubt, share the technology in question with your professor—you might actually end up teaching him or her something new! Bottom line: You cannot afford to be disorganized.

## Entering the Field

The field can be as far away as the other side of the world, or as close as your own community; in fact, some anthropologists insist on conducting local fieldwork:

> You discover that people in your neighborhood have widely divergent interests, do their shopping in very different places, watch very different TV channels, and talk with accents you never picked up before. Societies are a patchwork of micro-units; they only *look* homogenous. Second, as a fieldworker, you tend to start asking questions no one normally asks; you tend to establish connections between the here-and-now and other contexts, connections that no

one ever established; you tend to problematise things that nobody ever calls into question (and you problematise them perhaps precisely because of that). In other words, you have a very different orientation towards social reality, one that takes nothing for granted and which treats everything which is considered "normal" as suspect, intriguing and worthy of some investigation. (Blommaert and Jie 2010, 41–42)

One reason that professors assign you to study your own community is logistics: Studying your community is cost-effective and convenient. Studying your community can also

## Completing Research with "Human Subjects"

Completing these assignments might require you or your instructor to obtain Institutional Review Board (IRB) approval before entering the field. In some cases, your instructor might have already obtained approval for the students in the class to collect certain kinds of data, such as one-on-one interviews. In other cases, you will need to submit the paperwork. It is important not to deviate from what you are being permitted to do. For example, if your assignment is an observation of people at a public park, you are not allowed to interview them. Interviewing is a separate research activity requiring IRB approval based on informed consent, a description of the research and any benefits or risks incurred by participating in the research. This is so that the potential participant understands the study before giving consent, usually by signing a consent form.

be enlightening—remember, ethnographic work is *interpretive*. You are being asked to find meanings instead of truth (Ladner 2014). This means you need to embrace bias (Wolcott 1995); this is the reflexivity concept that was first mentioned in Chapter 1.

## Collecting Data and Taking Detailed Notes

Data collection might include photography, drawings, audio and video recordings, and written notes. It might also include quantitative data, which allows for some precision in observation but is at risk for biases due to time of day, observer effects, and seasonal and spatial effects (Mulder et al. 1985). And your data might also include trash, as Blommaert and Jie (2010) and other anthropologists have suggested—oh yes, especially trash. Each of these techniques has its own important advantages and limitations.

Here are some kinds of data you could collect:

| | |
|---|---|
| stories | interviews |
| forms | jokes |
| memos, notices | maps of places |
| graffiti | conversations |
| newspapers | meeting minutes |

In most cases, the most inconspicuous way to take fieldnotes is with pencil and a small bound notebook. You do not have to be high-tech about how you record your notes. Technology is great, but you will not be able to use it in all situations. For example, it is against the law to record or photograph people in a clinic waiting room because it violates their health privacy.

If you are writing about a single event, you will take a lot of notes in a short period of time. Record your expectations for the event before it starts. Have a picture of how you think the

## Common Problems with Student-Generated Fieldnotes

1. Relying on your memory instead of writing notes to recreate the sequence of events
2. Collecting too many details—more details means more analysis!
3. Writing too much about details that seem extraneous to the reader because they are left unexplained.
4. Selectively omitting information from the overall picture (this is a problem of *accuracy*).

event will happen. Take thorough notes during the event, even though you might be interacting and participating in the event at the same time. Some points you might consider include describing are as follows:

*Setting*: Describe the place and space where the observation is being conducted. Writing "the room was crowded" is less useful than "people were standing shoulder to shoulder and individuals encountered difficulty moving through the crowd from one end of the room to the other."

*Timing*: If you are conducting a timed observation with regular intervals when you are observing, use a watch or phone to record the time. Think about the context: How is the space you are observing different at different times of the day?

*Human physical characteristics:* As best you can, describe the age, gender, height, size, race and/or ethnicity, and clothing of the individuals you are observing.

*Objects*: Describe the presence, arrangement, and use of objects that the individuals you observe are using. What objects are the individuals using and why? Try to theorize about how the objects represent the broader values and beliefs held by the individuals.

*Use of language*: Listen carefully to what is being said, the context in which it is being said, and the volume and tone of conversation among participants. Record exact dialog as best you can. Note sarcasm and silences as well as other kinds of paralanguage, such as pitch, speed, pauses, and sighs.

*Nonverbal body movements*: Look at distances between people, their body postures, and their facial expressions. Do the movements match or contradict the words people are saying? Instead of making generalizations, such as "Most of the people seemed happy," document what people are actually *doing*. To say that everyone was wearing "brightly colored clothes" is less appropriate to fieldnotes than saying "The women all wore dresses, most in bright hues of red, yellow, and blue; the men wore black pants and shirts with bold, geometric patterns, mostly red and green." Instead of writing "The men were very angry," write what you see and hear: "Two in the corner started raising their voices, saying

Words like "happy," "beautiful," "emotional," "good," "bad," "intense," "boring," "hot," "cool," "tall," and the like are both abstract and relative—they can mean different things to different people. Instead, *describe* the scene, the people, and their actions with *sensory details*. Use all five senses: Describe sights, sounds, smells, tastes, and touch.

'That is not what I meant!' and one then poked the other in the chest." After the description, you can then add your interpretation, "They all seemed to be getting angry," but do that only *after* you have documented the scene in sensory detail.

*Sequence of events*: Identify behavioral patterns to understand the context for why the event looks the way it does. Who is performing the behavior? How often does the behavior occur? Does the behavior seem to vary by gender, race, or class? Pay attention to power differentials. Who seems to dictate the action, if anyone? Who speaks? Who doesn't? Are these behaviors part of a ritual? When does the ritual begin and end?

*Materials*: Look at the materials you could collect. What could each tell you?

Afterward, write your initial reactions immediately after the event has ended; how different are the expectations from what you observed? Recognize that your reflections consist of personal (emotional) and intellectual responses that might not be easy to separate. Writing fieldnotes can be such a personal exercise that many anthropologists treat their fieldnotes as private, like a diary (Blommaert and Jie 2010).

Here's an example from my fieldnotes during my first full day in the field in Guadeloupe, French West Indies:

I knew that the plumber was coming today to fix the toilet, and I figured I'd get up right before he came. Two youngish men came in a van. I thought it was funny that he introduced himself as "his name, Mr. Le Plombier" ("Mister the Plumber")—very French—and his assistant, who had an odd handshake. He put out his wrist instead of his hand and then I had to move my hand underneath his to actually shake it.

If I had stopped at "odd handshake," I would not be taking good fieldnotes because "odd" is not specific enough—in fact, it is a highly relative adjective because what seems odd to you might not seem odd to me. Documenting the nature of the handshake in ways that another reader could see (and that I could remember accurately later) was important. In fact, it wasn't until two weeks later that I saw this gesture again, this time by a bartender at a restaurant saying hello to his friend. One of my new friends explained to me that making physical contact with someone familiar is important as a greeting, but if your hands are dirty, you do not shake hands, you offer the wrist, elbow, whatever is clean. This is why the plumber's assistant offered his wrist instead of his hand; he had already been working that day. Not offering a dirty hand is a sign of respect, but making initial physical contact with the person as a greeting is still important. The lesson here is that when you write your fieldnotes, record every gesture, no matter how small.

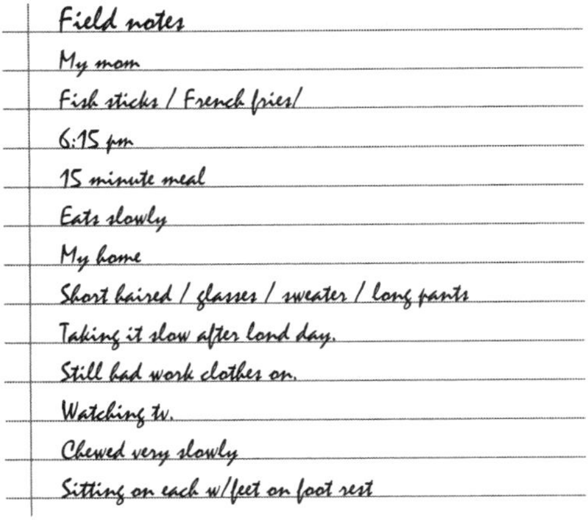
Field notes
My mom
Fish sticks / French fries/
6:15 pm
15 minute meal
Eats slowly
My home
Short haired / glasses / sweater / long pants
Taking it slow after lond day.
Still had work clothes on.
Watching tv.
Chewed very slowly
Sitting on each w/feet on foot rest

FIGURE 3.2 An All-Too-Brief List of "Fieldnotes".

Here's an example of incomplete fieldnotes written by a student completing an assignment where the person observes someone eating.

The notes entered here seem like placeholders for things to be elaborated on later, but the student never does elaborate. These are not good fieldnotes because he is relying too much on his memory. For example, "15-minute meal" is entered on one line, but there is no detail about how the person ate, or where. Duration is important, and the time, logged as 6:15pm, could give hints about this being a dinnertime meal. But from this short list of notes, the student was not able to provide in-depth details, which provoke unanswered questions and lost points:

- Where did this meal happen?
- How was the meal eaten (by hand? with utensils? what kind? speed?)
- Is she eating alone? Might this affect how someone eats?
- What does "taking it slow" look like? What do "your mom's" work clothes look like? The student knows, but the reader wouldn't.

Let's look at some observation fieldnotes as well. We'll start with a less successful excerpt of an observation of a basketball game.

During the game there were several observations I made in regards to my senses. In terms of sound, there was the chanting and cheering from the crowed, as well as music being played over the PA system. In addition, you could often hear the players on the court yelling plays to each other or calling for the ball, and coaches yelling out instructions to their team. There was also the ever-present sound of basketball sneakers squeaking on the hardwood court, which initially was quite grating, but the squeaking quickly faded into the ambient noise of the arena. The only smells I noticed were the smells of the food that the people in my section were eating. I smelled different types of foods, including hotdogs, chicken tenders, and french fries, but the food that smelled the strongest was the popcorn, whose buttery aroma could be smelled from quite far away and permeated the arena. In terms of sight, there were many things to focus on; of course, the game unfolding on the court, as well as the big screen where they would show replays and fan-cams. During halftime, I enjoyed watching the halftime entertainment where they had two young kids get dressed into oversized team uniforms and then score a basket for prizes.

← The original assignment must have asked student writers to provide details by reminding them of their senses. This is a heavy-handed paragraph listing each sense and what he associates with them, as if he's trying to cover his bases, instead of letting the thick description happen organically. The student makes this a paragraph about everything happening with the senses, on the basketball court and in the stands near him, and the result is that the paragraph reads in an unfocused way. Also, this is only description, not analysis.

This next excerpt is very good and comes from a student writing about a dyadic interaction, an interaction between two people. In this case, a mother and son are waiting in line at a café.

At approximately 12:15 pm, my attention was drawn to a small boy at the end of the café line, repeatedly yelling "Mom! Mom! Mom!" The boy must have been around five years old and wore blue jeans, a navy-blue down jacket, a white undershirt, and a green baseball cap. Towering over him was his mother, a tall woman with brown wavy hair that barely reached her shoulders. She looked like she was in her mid-thirties and wore a long white winter coat with black pants and flat black boots. She carried a large brown bag that she struggled to keep over her right shoulder. The café line was growing shorter and the boy seemed energetic as he continuously bobbed up and down on the tip of his toes. The mother opened the large bag to retrieve her cell phone, answering the call in a loud, quick-paced tone. As she spoke on the phone, her son tugged at the bottom of her coat and again shouted, "Mom! Mom! Mom!" The mother waved her right hand toward her son as if flicking a fly off of her coat. From this gesture, I could tell she was growing annoyed by her son's persistence and impatience. The boy struggled to gain her attention, so he started to pull on the black rope that sectioned off the café line. The rope's pole began to rock back-and-forth, until the mother snapped her phone shut, grabbed her son by the sleeve and demanded, "You need to behave, Mister." The boy looked pleased since he had regained his mother's attention. The boy was clearly upset that his mother was not paying complete attention to him.

← Notice that the student writer uses very detailed descriptions of the clothing the two people wore, as well as the boy's increasing pestering of his mother as she continues to ignore him. The writer builds on the paragraph so that its climax is the dialog between them. Overall, this student does an excellent job of description, but she leaves her analysis of the interaction to the last two sentences.

Finally, here is a more successful excerpt about another interaction between two people at a café. The assignment asked students to ascertain the relationship between the people based on their body language.

As they walked towards the door to the café the girl laughed showing her teeth and the boy was smiling. The girl then flicked her hair over her shoulder to my left and they continued walking towards me (the café).

When they reach the glass door the guy reached his hand up over the girl's head to open it for her and she slipped under his arm in through the door. He followed her past the coffee machines and into the main aisle down the center of the café. Their laughter had faded now and they looked more serious. There was no more conversation as the guy followed her to the aisle and then they walked out of the café into the library. During this time there was no exchange of conversation or affection between the two. As they proceeded down the aisle the boy quickened his pace to walk next to the girl again. The conversation resumed and I heard her remark "Have you seen [John]?" To this the boy lifted his head up slightly as though to think before replying "Nah, I do not know what he's been up to." To this the girl simply laughed quietly a little and flicked her hair over her shoulder saying, "I miss him, he's so funny!" before they were out of earshot and almost out of Bookworms. When they were almost out of eyesight the girl pulled out her phone and looked down at it quickly pressing buttons with her fingers and slowing her pace.

← Notice that the student writer includes both dialog and body language. She was smart to choose two people who were close enough that she could see and hear them.

While this exchange was very short I can deduce some information from it. First of all the two people above mentioned had some kind of relationship, but it is nearly impossible to say whether it was simply friendship or study partners or even dating. The lack of affection leads me to believe it is more likely a friendship or study relationship since they were at the library. The dress of the girl leans towards the idea that she cares about her appearance since she wears trendy brands and her jeans with boots looked put together. The guy seems to care less since he was in sweats. In addition, I believe the girl to be more

← Here, the student is making inferences about the power dynamic between the two people; she also uses the context of the library café to provide guesses about the relationship between them. She is unsure if they're friends or study partners or are dating. She seems comfortable in the ambiguity.

dominant than the boy because she navigated the coffee pots and he followed. The male also seems to be a gentleman because he held the door. The short conversation leads me to believe they were mentioning a mutual friend and the girl's laughter perhaps they he had done something embarrassing lately most likely drunk. Last, the girl doing what seemed to be texting on her phone makes me think she was meeting friends or other people to study since she pulled out her phone upon entering the library entrance and began pressing buttons; however she could be replying to a text as well.

From this observation I believe I learned to pay more attention to the small details of what people do and how they do it. While the short time period made it hard to take in-depth notes to later analyze I believe I worked well with the materials I had. This experiment was a success to me because I completed the assignment and managed not to feel completely awkward during it.

The lesson here is "make the familiar strange." When you think like an anthropologist in the field, you make the familiar strange, to recall Chapter 1; you lay aside your assumptions about the world around you and attempt to see things, objects, behaviors, and people in context and in real time. You might think that because you are observing something that is mundane to you, such as having dinner with your friends, you fully understand everything. Following Clifford Geertz, the idea is to see all of the possible meanings of a behavior and explain them in a way that a cultural outsider can understand.

## Conducting an Interview

You might have seen the phrase "ethnographic interview" before, but as Blommaert and Jie (2010, 42) argue, there is no such thing: "there is nothing intrinsically ethnographic about an interview, and doing interviews does not make your research ethnographic . . . research is ethnographic because it accepts a number of fundamental principles and views on social reality." The ethnographic interview simply provides you with more details for your overall study.

### Before the Interview—Develop an Interview Guide

Carefully consider your research questions and formulate the interview questions with ethnography in mind. You will also have to consider the "how" of the interview, the benefits and drawbacks of conducting face-to-face versus telephone or online interviews, and how to maintain some consistency so that the responses will not be biased as a result of how the data was collected.

- Make all questions relevant to the research question (Gorden 1992).
- Consider the fact that how you ask the question affects the kind of responses you will receive: closed-ended, open-ended, or a mixture of both. (See examples of questions below.)
- Include probing questions to obtain more details, providing opportunities for the participant to elaborate (examples: Could you tell me more? Could you give an example?).
- Avoid leading questions. Leading questions anticipate what the answer will be, thereby limiting the range of possible responses.
- Make sure to use words that the participant can understand—think about your audience as you develop questions.

## Examples of Questions Generated for a Survey Conducted by Telephone

How do you use telephones? (open-ended: allows the person to describe)

Do you use a cell phone? (closed-ended: prompts a yes/no answer)

How do you use your smartphone? (leading: assumes the person has a smartphone)

What kind of feedback do you want to receive by phone? (leading: assumes the person wants feedback)

## During the Interview—Let the Participant Talk

The single biggest mistake made by students conducting interviews is to talk too much. Your goal is to get data from your participant. You want to create a safe atmosphere so that your interviewee will provide you with good data, and then you want to let him or her talk.

- Explain the consent form and present it in writing to the potential participant. If the interview will be audio-recorded, show the person the recording device and check the audio.
- Conduct the interview in a space that is convenient, comfortable, and safe for the participant.
- Organize the interview so that it follows as closely as possible the parameters outlined in the consent form.
- Practice active listening to understand what the participant is saying. Ask immediate follow-up questions. Remain silent most of the time to allow the participant to speak.
- Thank the participant for his or her time and provide appropriate compensation (if outlined in the research protocol and consent form).

- Record your own notes about the interview immediately afterward.

## After the Interview—Analyze Your Notes

When using interviewing as a method, the analysis comes down to quotes as the "currency" (Ladner 2014). Emerson, Fretz, and Shaw (1995) describe the analytical process as having two parts: (1) reading the notes "as a complete corpus" and (2) analytically coding fieldnotes to identify patterns in the notes that develop into themes that can contribute to an overall understanding.

### Suggestions for Analyzing Transcribed Interview Data

Professional anthropologists have interviews transcribed, meaning that the audio file is converted to a written account of the interview. It is a tedious but necessary process. Every utterance could be important—these pauses and paralanguage are very important to linguistic anthropologists. To analyze the transcribed interview, they often use one of the following strategies:

1. Look at the transcript first as if it is a painting (Blommaert and Jie 2010) to identify pauses, interruptions, short, pithy responses, and long monologs.
2. Read the transcripts for content, noting patterns in phrases, terminology, and experiences in the responses.
3. Arrange recurring patterns in the responses into themes. Here they may draw a conceptual model or framework to explain the experiences.
4. Identify exemplary quotes that illustrate each theme.

Anthropologists analyze their data in as many ways as they collect it. Thus, there's no one way to analyze interviews, for example. Depending on the nature of the topic and how the interviews are collected, audio recording might not be possible. Transcription is useful for getting the exact words and pauses, especially if the interviews were conducted in one language and you need to translate them into another. Some anthropologists who *do* record interviews might not transcribe them but instead elect to listen to their interviews to verify something.

To identify salient patterns in the text and the themes that arise from the data you collect, try asking questions of your fieldnotes, as Emerson, Fretz, and Shaw (1995, 146) suggest:

- What are people doing? What are they trying to accomplish?
- How, exactly, do they do this? What specific means and/or strategies do they use?
- How do members talk about, characterize, and understand what is going on?
- What assumptions are they making?
- What do I see going on here? What did I learn from these notes?
- Why did I include them?

In the end, a good analysis of an interview both gives voice to the individual speakers and addresses the original research questions.

## Being Reflexive

As explained in "Expectations of Anthropological Writing" in Chapter 1, being reflexive means being aware of your

*Implicit bias* is a phrase from psychology used to point out that everyone carries preconceived notions that shape who people are and how they think. Anthropologists understand that ethnocentrism is the lens that everyone looks through.

relationship to what you are seeing. Four basic ways to be reflexive are as follows:

- Draw on your gut reaction to the event. That gut reaction is a visceral sense of things, things you cannot initially put into words. If you were pleased or repulsed by something, consider why you felt that way. Why did the event make you uneasy or comfortable? Question the *why* and *how* behind your emotional and intellectual responses. Keep in mind that extremes of "I loved it" or "I hated it" sound stale and commonplace. Draw out the emotion.
- Describe the sequence of events that you observed, and then analyze. Compare what you expected to what you actually observed. Look for *patterns*. Look for connections between your own perspective and what you observed, between the event or behavior and others, and between this event and related issues. Help your readers interpret the event in a way that goes beyond the obvious.
- Acknowledge your own ethnocentrism and identify ways to move past it. For cultural anthropologists, recognizing and moving through culture shock and all its uncomfortable stages is part of growth as a researcher; it is also considered an important part of showing that you have transcended the rite of passage of conducting fieldwork and that now you can competently conduct fieldwork throughout your career.

- Reflect on the experience. As part of the assignment, you might be asked to write a paragraph or two that contains a self-assessment of your ability to conduct this kind of fieldwork-based research. Your instructor is interested in what it is like for you to try to think and act like a budding anthropologist trying out new methods. What have you learned about yourself as a result of doing this assignment? Do not create a "I was blind but now I see" narrative because it is cloying. Instead, earnestly describe your strengths and weaknesses in approaching the assignment, what you noticed as potential ethical issues, and what you would do differently if you tried out this kind of method in the field again.

## Writing the Ethnography

Here's a secret: Anthropologists do not agree on how to structure an ethnography. There are several possible structures for writing the ethnography. Wolcott (2010) describes five possible organizing structures for presenting ethnographic data:

1. Case studies
2. Organizing by relevant themes (this technique is called thematic coding)
3. Describing a hierarchy within an organization and progressing through each layer
4. Organizing by groups of people, concerned parties, who contribute to the research question
5. Using the life story of one person as a way to illustrate important themes.

Students are often asked to write their ethnographies in one of two styles: essay format or in a scientific "IMRaD"

Keep in mind the main characteristics of a good ethnography, including a good mini-ethnography, according to Wolcott (2010):

1. Ethnography is holistic.
2. Ethnography is cross-cultural.
3. Ethnography is comparative.
4. Ethnography is authentic.
5. Ethnography is real.
6. Ethnography requires intimate, long-term acquaintance.
7. Ethnography is non-judgmental.
8. Ethnography is descriptive.
9. Ethnography is specific.
10. Ethnography is flexible, adaptive.
11. Ethnography is corroborative.
12. Ethnography is idiosyncratic and individualistic.

format. Both formats are described in more detail in Chapter 5. Regardless of format, you must keep participants safe; use pseudonyms for your participants or assign study identification numbers. Consider using other privacy strategies (de-identifying data, secure storage of paper like notes and printouts). It is not just good practice for writing up research, but IRBs may also insist on it.

## Essay Format

With this structure, you would write a narrative of the observation from start to finish. In the first two paragraphs you would describe the setting and duration of the observations, and in the body paragraphs you would discuss your fieldnotes—that is, what was observed. You might go point by point and pepper your observations with analysis and interpretations, or you could save it all for the final paragraphs.

## IMRD Format

You can find this format, which is outlined in Chapter 5, in some anthropology journals, and the degree to which the text has a narrative style varies. The *introduction* provides an objective, theoretical framework. The *methods* section contains the "who, what, where" of the observation. Be specific about the dates and times of the observation. For longer fieldwork experiences, such as weeks or months, describe the total duration of time spent in the field. The *results* section focuses on describing your findings. Here, in detailing the accuracy of your findings, you convey your expertise and trustworthiness to your readers. Finally, the *discussion* section focuses on interpreting your findings. Consider the following questions:

- What is the meaning of what you have observed?
- How do the observations compare to the expected phenomena? Why do you think what you observed happened?
- Are there any connections or patterns in what you observed?
- Did the stated or implicit objectives of what you were observing match what was achieved?
- What were the strengths and weaknesses of your fieldnotes (or other data collection technique)?
- What have you learned from what you observed?

The bottom line is that you can be creative with this kind of assignment, even though you should check with your professor to make sure that you are staying within the boundaries of the assignment.

# REVIEWING
# THE LITERATURE

A literature review is a comprehensive synthesis of previously published research on a specific topic or research question. The literature review is the most versatile writing genre in anthropology because identifying, evaluating, and using sources will help you to prepare research papers, research reports, and proposals, all of which have literature review sections (whether formally labeled as such or not).

Some students think of a literature review as picking a topic, plugging terms into a search engine, finding articles, and then writing up summaries of them, but it is more than that. As the diagram shows, the literature review is a critical piece that requires the writer to take a stand on an issue and collect already published work that supports the argument. Think of the literature review as a search for *relationships* and *trends* in a coherent set of research sources.

The literature review might be an entire research project in itself or just the introductory section of a research report or proposal. It is intended to "expose the reviewing scientist to the past, current, and ongoing research about a subject the scientist is exploring for future research of his or her own" (Schmidt, Smyth, and Kowalski 2014, 37).

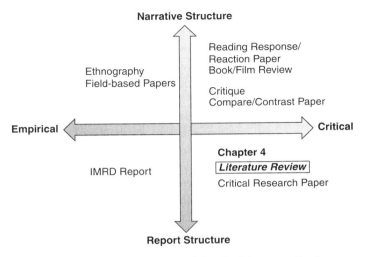

FIGURE 4.1  Structure and Approach for the Literature Review.

Your review should be guided by the assumption that no academic field is static; instead it is a series of controversies and conversations. Therefore, you should not set out to *solve* or *prove* anything in your literature review (indeed, you should avoid the word "prove" in anthropology writing). There may be subtle differences in the way an archaeologist would want to see a literature review compared to the way a linguistic anthropologist would want to see it, so check with your instructor for any discipline-specific conventions.

The information in this chapter could also be used to write an annotated bibliography. The annotated bibliography paper is a variation of the literature review; instead of writing an essay with introductory, concluding, and body paragraphs, the bibliography reads like a catalog of entries connected by a research question. For an annotated bibliography, you will need to understand the article thoroughly to write your own

> **Literature reviews are useful for:**
>
> - Catching up on the essential background, context, and research consensus on a topic
> - Showing that you are a competent, critical researcher
> - Identifying relevant questions, key terms, relationships, and trends
> - Identifying gaps in knowledge
> - "Unpacking" a conceptual framework
> - Gathering evidence for your argument
> - Understanding the most relevant counter-arguments
> - Setting up the rest of the research paper/proposal

abstract of it and evaluate it. So, annotated bibliographies consist of four major steps: (1) finding the sources, (2) annotating them, (3) summarizing and evaluating them, and then (4) explaining how each source fits into your research topic.

## Finding a Promising Topic

The first step in writing a literature review is to identify a topic—that is, unless you have been assigned one. Review these sets of sample topics:

|  | Topic Specificity Level 1 | Topic Specificity Level 2 | Topic Specificity Level 3 |
| --- | --- | --- | --- |
| Example 1 | Neanderthals | Evidence of Neanderthal culture | Mousterian stone tool tradition, the oldest Neanderthal tool tradition |

| | Topic Specificity Level 1 | Topic Specificity Level 2 | Topic Specificity Level 3 |
|---|---|---|---|
| Example 2 | Shark fin soup | Conservation and controversy in eating shark fin soup | Genetic sequencing and identification of hammerhead shark fins used in shark fin soup |

Most students identify a topic, find out how much information there is on that topic, and then decide on the topic. If you are not sure of your topic, aim for level 2 specificity when you conduct your preliminary search: specific enough to make the number of search results manageable, but broad enough to give yourself some options.

But you do not have to go it alone: Share your topic early with your professor and/or a librarian and ask for feedback so that you are not floundering for too long.

## Searching for Articles

Once you have your topic, you will need to search in the right databases for research to include in your literature review. Here is a good opportunity to discuss interdisciplinarity, the crossing of academic boundaries to incorporate the work of other academic fields or the collaboration of multiple researchers with different academic techniques and expertise to approach a problem[1]. Anthropologists have been working this way long before other scholars caught on. As noted in Chapter 1, anthropology is *holistic*, meaning anthropologists do not limit themselves to the research of other anthropologists. Depending on the topic, they seek relevant research from history, gender studies, sociology, rural studies, geography, medicine, and many other fields.

The reflex to search with Google is perhaps so automatic that you will do it first no matter what, so go ahead. But then try

Google Scholar, which will limit your results to academic sources. But even if you gather more than the minimum number of sources required by your instructor from those simple searches, if you stop there, you will not have done a real literature review. And even if you further search general databases like Academic Search Premier or Scopus that you may be familiar with from doing research in first-year writing and other courses, you will not have done a thorough enough literature review. You must also engage with the specialized databases of the field, particularly Anthrosource and Anthropology Plus. Consult your library's website—or even better, flesh-and-blood librarians—to learn how to access these.

When you search in a database, you need to search in a way that that specific database accepts search terms—few of them work like Google. If you are having trouble finding relevant sources, that might be because:

- You are asking a research question that is too specific
- The topic is not relevant to anthropology (but surprise! Everything is anthropology)
- You are not using terminology specific to anthropology
- You are not taking alternate spellings into account (e.g., Chanukah, Hanukkah, and other versions)
- You are not using Boolean operators (and, or, not) correctly.

Try changing the keywords—this may take 10 or 20 tries with different keywords. If you find too much, however, use limiters[2]: filter by date or article type (peer-reviewed only), or narrow your topic.

Let's say your topic is on Neanderthals and evidence of culture. A classic mistake is to try to search only for your search terms and then give up when you do not find what you thought was out there. Instead, develop a family of related terms. Below are two families of search terms: one for Neanderthal culture and another for the controversy surrounding shark fin soup (it is a delicacy for

Chinese people but is becoming increasingly expensive and in some cases illegal because of worries that the shark population is decreasing because of the shark fin trade).

| Do Not Just Search for... | Also Try These |
| --- | --- |
| Neanderthal culture | Neandertal, *Homo neanderthalensis* (alternative, scientific spellings) |
| | Neanderthal behavior, culture |
| | names of sites where Neanderthal fossils have been found |
| | tool use |
| | teeth wear/dentition |
| | use of fire |
| Shark fin soup | Chinese delicacies |
| | banned foods, shark fin controversy |
| | legal bans on sale and trade of shark fin |
| | shark fin harvesting practices |
| | Chinese tradition |
| | sustainable harvesting |
| | shark fin substitute |

Remember to look for books, too, which you should do by searching your library's catalog as well as the anthropology-specific databases (you can even use Amazon.com as a shortcut for searching for books).

For both books and articles, *mine their lists of references.* The references section of both books and articles give clues to the "bibliographical trails"[3] that authors make, and it is perfectly fine—even an excellent research habit—to use the reference section of one article to look for similar articles that might fit your research question. Also pay attention to

There's no shame in struggling to find the most relevant sources. Even experienced researchers occasionally run into dead ends and get frustrated when searching for sources. When they do, they turn to librarians. Novices often want to go it alone, so they avoid the librarians; they see seeking one out as a sign of weakness. But, in fact, consulting with a librarian a sign of *strength* and *maturity* as a researcher. At any point in your research process, seek out a librarian—preferably a specialist in the social sciences, which most college libraries have— and ask him or her for assistance. This is the reference librarians' job, and most of them like that job. They *want* you to seek them out. Fifteen minutes consulting with a reference librarian can save you hours of lonely, unfruitful research time.

whether certain titles keep coming up again and again in the reference sections of the articles and books you are finding. This is an indicator that that source is important, a touchstone that all the insiders know, so you too should probably seek it out and read it.

## Looking for Relationships and Patterns

Once you have read several sources, start looking for relationships and patterns. Check with the assignment first to see if there are clues about how to organize the literature review. You may need to create charts to help convey your findings to readers. Hubbuch[4] offers the following suggestions for analyzing your notes:

- What theory or theories seem to be the most popular? Which theories are referred to most often? Hint: Anthropologists use active verbs when discussing theory, such as "employ," "assess," "develop," and "critique." Here is an example from the abstract of the research article "Ontological anthropology and the deferral of critique" by Bessire and Bond[5]: "we develop an ethnographic and theoretical critique of ontological anthropology." Which theories are the basis for most of the studies or experiments you looked at? Has there been a shift in the popularity of theories?

- What basic assumptions do most of the researchers seem to be making about the subject?
- Can you categorize the research reports you have read according to the test procedures used in the studies/experiments?
- Can you categorize the research reports you have read according to the kinds of subjects or material tested or observed?
- Can you see any patterns in the results reported?
- Are there any patterns in the conclusions drawn by the researchers?
- What experts' names pop up most frequently? Are certain experts associated with certain types of research, certain theories, certain areas of investigation?

Once you find some articles that closely fit your topic, you should conduct citation searching:

- Look for additional recent or previous articles by the authors of that article.
- Look for additional articles that cite that article.
- Look at the references of that article and look to see who else cited them.
- Look at what else those other authors have published.

By looking forward and backward in time from the publication date of the source you found, you get a cross-section of the key authors and seminal works on your topic. To be thorough, stay organized and keep track of the sources you find—this is how you build competence as a researcher and avoid becoming someone who claims, "There is little information on this topic" or "This topic is understudied" when that is just not true.

## Setting Inclusion Criteria for Choosing Articles Relevant to Your Topic

For everything you read, you should develop a battery of questions that you would regularly ask any text. These questions will help you identify which of the many articles you'll find deserve further investigation:

- Who is the author?
- How logical is the author's reasoning?
- Where is the piece published, by whom, and why? Note: Not all secondary sources are made equally. Peer-reviewed literature is at the top of the hierarchy because it must meet the standards of peer review (being judged by the experts in the field as being worthy of publication). Tips for doing

### Invite in the Troublemakers

When searching for sources, be sure to include some that *challenge* what you want to say or that supply counter-arguments to your emerging argument. Remember, you are supposed to capture the *controversies* on your topic, and you can't do that if you only select sources that align with one point of view. Literature reviews are *stronger* when they include studies that challenge the consensus, point out limitations, and challenge your own emerging argument or thesis. These lend energy (not to mention honesty) to reviews.

an effective classroom peer review are in the Appendix. Newspapers and magazines, by contrast, constitute popular literature; the publications are still checked by editors, but the level of scrutiny is lower and the intended audience is different.

- How current is the article? Note: Currency is subjective based on your topic and how you narrow your focus. For example, computer science articles from 1962 are totally out of date, but so are some articles from only two years ago.
- What seems to be the writer's purpose? That is, what is the paper *doing*?
- What is the evidence being presented? Is this evidence valid?
- What are any alternative explanations for the results?

## Some Other Important Questions to Ask

*How does this article fit your topic?*
- Do not be afraid to discard it if not relevant.

*How does it relate to the other sources I have already read?*
- Does it affirm the consensus? Offer a counter-view? Introduce new methods?

*What biases are present in the article?*
- What theoretical approach does the author use? Does this approach affect what the researcher chose to focus on? What assumptions does the author make?

*How does this article fit into broader issues of anthropology, such as inequality?*

## Reading to Extract Key Information from the Articles You Choose

When you find a research article that you believe fits your criteria, you need to evaluate the merits of the publication for your topic.

### Look at the *Sections* of the Article

Some readers might read the first paragraph or two of the introduction, but most experienced academic readers go straight to the findings section and look at any figures and tables—any visuals that convey knowledge. What are the names of the headings? What are the topic sentences?

### Take in the Overview

Take lots of notes, but get into the habit of writing the notes in your own words to reduce the risk of plagiarism when you paraphrase. Make note of what the author's main argument is; you are going to need this if you end up citing him or her. Anthropologists like to create new words and phrases. What key terms stand out? You do not want to misrepresent the author's ideas just to fit your paper. The original context of a source is important for understanding the source, and prevents quoting out of context, so identify the argument and any key themes when you skim[3].

### Ask Key Questions

Schmidt, Smyth, and Kowalski[2] suggest asking the following six questions about the study (and finding the answers in the text). Notice how these questions are as much about the *context*, *purpose*, and *methods* as they are about the content. Novice readers tend to ask, "What are the main points?" and stop there. Experienced readers ask that, but first and foremost ask, "Why did the authors write this article—what's their purpose?" and these additional questions (Schmidt, Smyth, and Kowalski 2014, 100):

1.  What is the question, controversy, or problem driving the study? *(Find in the Title or Introduction)*
2.  Who or what group was being studied? Describe these people as much as possible, including their location(s), their characteristic(s), and their condition(s). *(Find in the Methodology or Procedures)*
3.  How was the study executed? (What method was used, what kind of study was done?) *(Find in the Methodology)*
4.  What questions were addressed or asked in the study to generate data? *(Find in the Methodology and Results of Research)*
5.  What was found in the study? What were the results of the study? Why did the scientists think they found what they found? *(Find in the Results of Research and Analysis)*
6.  After looking at the Results and Analysis, compare and contrast the studies. This comparison and contrast will become your analysis. Are they similar or different? What are the similarities among the studies and what are the differences? Are the questions driving the study similar? Are the groups studied similar or different? Are the results of the studies similar or different? Are there similar analyses of the findings? Are there trends in the various aspects of the studies, omissions, errors, or elements of the studies that are difficult to understand or rationalize?

To model how an experienced reader might approach a peer-reviewed journal article, let's take a look at Lynnette Arnold's 2012 article in the *Journal of Linguistic Anthropology*, "Reproducing actions, reproducing power: Local ideologies and everyday practices of participation at a California community bike shop."

## First Look at the Title and Identify Its Key Words

In this case, those are *power, ideologies, reproducing,* and *everyday practices*; perhaps *community bike shop* is also a key word/phrase since that is the site of the study.

## Review the Abstract

In this case, that reads: "The study of participation within linguistic anthropology has developed a nuanced understanding of participant roles and examined the process by which such roles are enacted in participation frameworks. This paper examines what I call modes of engagement, that is, role-based differential use of forms of embodied and linguistic participation. I argue that such engagement modes are central in defining and differentiating participant roles themselves. The analysis focuses on data gathered at a bilingual bicycle-repair shop with an overtly prescriptive ideology of participation. Ethnographic and interactional analysis demonstrates that such ideologies both influence and are shaped by local practices, and have material consequences for who can participate and how they do so."

## Examine the Structure

It is written in a IMRD (Introduction/Methods/Results/Discussion) format, but the headings are descriptive—that is, the first two headings are "Participation and Power" and "Participant Roles, Modes of Engagement, and Ideologies of Appropriateness" instead of "Introduction." There are several figures, tables, and photographs providing demographic information about the participants and dialogs between the people at the bike shop matched to their gestures. Here, the linguistic anthropologist is using combinations of word choice, word order, and body language to reveal something about the speakers and the situation in which their conversations are occurring.

## Identify the Purpose

Often an author comes right out and states the purpose of the article, as in this sentence from the first paragraph of the bike shop article: "In this article, I analyze the enactment and implications of this normative participation model in which particular participant roles were defined primarily by reference to specific forms of embodied engagement, illustrating how such expectations were creatively taken up, reproduced, and resisted."

## Ask the Essential Questions

### What is the Question, Controversy, or Problem Driving the Study?

You typically find this in the title or introduction. Look for sentences with pointers: "The main idea of the study is" or "The purpose is" or "In this article I argue . . ." Here's a quote from the second paragraph that points to the author's argument: "This article argues that everyday participation practices are critically impacted by, and constitutive of, social inequality and power. The analysis reveals that, despite the bike shop's well-intentioned goal of egalitarian empowerment, the contextualized implementation of this ideology of participation unwittingly reinforced the very social, economic, racial, and linguistic inequalities that the organization was dedicated to addressing." A possible paraphrase of this passage could be: *The bike shop is designed to be a place for everyone, but the ways that the volunteer bike mechanics and the community members spoke to each other reflect power differences that reinforce existing community disparities that the shop was trying to reduce.*

### Who or What Group was Being Studied?

Describe these people as much as possible, including their location(s), their characteristic(s), and their condition(s). The most basic answer that is still completely accurate is: Volunteer bike mechanics and community members who use a bilingual nonprofit bike shop in California called Bica Lo-Teca. An experienced reader would also point out how the volunteers describe how they teach community members (hands-off, verbal instruction) and that the interactions and words used reflect issues of power between the two groups.

### How was the Study Executed? What Method was Used? What Kind of Study was Done?

The following information comes from the subsection titled "Participation in Context" located on the fifth page of the article: three months of regular biweekly participant observation during Open Shop sessions in fall 2009, photo documentation of the physical space of the shop, five audio-recorded ethnographic interviews with staff and volunteers, ranging from 45 to 90 minutes in length, and about 15 hours of video-recorded footage of interaction. Depending on how the research articles are structured, information on methodology could be in a section plainly titled "Methods" or a section with a more descriptive title. You may have to dig a little to find this information in a typical cultural anthropology article, but it will appear before the presentation of the research findings.

### What Questions were Addressed or Asked in the Study to Generate Data?

This question is not as easy to answer directly because the interview questions aren't provided, but the tables with the dialogs provide information about the interactions the author wants the reader to understand.

### What was Found in the Study? What were the Results of the Study? Why did the Scientists Think they Found what they Found?

Look near the beginning of the section called "Introducing the Ideology of Participation to Newcomers." This section explains that the volunteers found it sometimes funny that newcomers to the shop did not realize that they would be learning to do their own bike repair rather than have the volunteer mechanic do the work. Look for places where the author's voice is evident and comments on the results that have been presented. Here's a spot later in the same section: "The erasure of differences between participants resulted in an unwitting reproduction of just those social, economic, and linguistic hierarchies that Bica's goal of egalitarian empowerment sought to weaken. The model of participation espoused by Bica Lo-Teca thus constituted a paradox of sorts for participants in the Open Shop community of practice, as they attempted to maintain egalitarianism in the context of an ideology of participation that authorized asymmetrical relationships between participants. As a result, volunteers sought to soften and minimize their impositions on shop users . . ." The author is *synthesizing* the findings to come to some conclusions about them.

### How does this Study—in its Methods as Well as in the Findings it Shares—Relate to other Relevant or Potential Studies?

For example, you might ask in this particular case: How is the situation at Bica Lo-Teca similar to or different from situations identified in other studies that examine other small businesses or community groups? What are other ways that power emerges (or doesn't emerge) through language in the other studies? Are the groups studied similar or different? What are the similarities and differences in the experiences of the Bica Lo-Teca volunteer bike mechanics and community members? Do the other studies you have identified make interesting parallels? How would it be different if the volunteer bike mechanics were paid employees? Would it make a difference if this were a floral shop instead of a bike shop? Are Arnold's research questions similar to the research questions in the other studies? Are the results of the studies similar or different? Are there similar analyses of the findings? For example, do other studies use participant observation or other methods? Are there trends in the various aspects of the studies, omissions, errors, or elements of the studies that are difficult to understand or rationalize? These kinds of questions show an active mind at work. Your job in a literature review is not to simply show that you have read the requisite number of articles but to ask those kinds of questions, to be an active mind at work.

## Developing Your Argument

Literature reviews are exploratory because you first need to read up on your topic to have something intelligent to say about it. To move from a series of summaries to an argument, ask yourself the following:

- What is my specific problem or research question?
- How does each source relate to it?
- What type of literature review am I conducting?
- Am I seeing trends in theory, in methods, within the work of specific researchers, in findings across sources? What can I say about the trend?
- What unexpected findings or patterns emerged as I read across the literature?
- Are there contradictions or telling points of disagreement in the literature?
- Where do I stand on the specific debates under way among the authors of the sources?

If you are expected to use your literature review in service to a thesis-driven critical research essay, you should turn to Chapter 5 to discover strategies for developing that kind of thesis and argument. If your task is more narrowly defined as a literature review, you may not need to assert a thesis, but you should still do *synthesis*—that is, move beyond a series of dutiful summaries. The questions above, as well as the section below, can help you do that.

## Structuring the Review

Literature reviews have the following macro-sections, even when they are not labeled exactly this way:

- Introduction
- Body with section headings by topic, chronology, or populations studied
- Conclusions

### Introduction

The introduction should explain the reason why the literature review is being conducted. Sometimes, the statement of the objective comes near the end of the introduction, after you have given some background and context. For example: "For the last twenty-five years, medical anthropologists have ascribed to critical medical anthropology as a theoretical model . . ." This sentence provides a decent foundation for the direction of the literature review, but do not be overbroad. Do not be afraid to state the objective plainly: "The objective of this article is to . . ." Here's an example from the first two sentences of a 2001 review by Bonanno and Constance in *Culture & Agriculture* on Fordism (industrialized mass production) applied to agriculture:

> The objective of this article is to map out the now large literature on Fordism, its crisis, and the transition toward post-Fordism and/or Globalization as it pertains

to agriculture and food. The idea is to systematize the significant body of knowledge that has been produced in the last two decades by scholars whose aim was to investigate global trends and their impact on the agricultural and food sectors.

The next sentences should summarize what the researchers you are presenting have been trying to investigate ("The primary motivations behind their studies were to . . ." or "Researchers have documented . . ."). Then introduce your argument in one or two sentences. This style of writing requires you to present the literature, not yourself, so although you might find "I" statements in a published literature review (such as "I argue," "I present"), you should use them sparingly in your own writing—unless it is common in the style of the audience you are writing for. Here's an excerpt from Kenneth McGill's (2013, E84) introduction to a literature review about political economy and language:

I therefore seek to establish a set of "particular and relational meanings" which are relevant to this line of scholarship. By examining the terms commodity, economic resource, instrumentality, social distinction and ideology, I hope to suggest some of the ways in which it is possible to continue to explore the relationship between language and political economy in a fruitful manner, and especially to encourage more linguistic anthropologists to engage with this expanding literature.

Notice the use of the present tense here.

You may want to include some limitations up front, so that you acknowledge you may not have found every single source, but it is not necessary. Here's how Bonanno and Constance (2001, 1) did it:

> We very much support the idea that dialogue between those who study the macro dimensions of agriculture and food and those who concentrate on the study of its micro dimensions is one of the most important scientific enterprises of our time. With all this said, we would like to underscore that the systematization of this literature required simplification that, while capturing the essential messages of these contributions, often does not do justice to this very rich and stimulating body of knowledge.

Finally, forecast how your literature review is organized: "Research on this topic is/can be organized into the following (number) categories:" and then list the heading names. You can even use numbers in your list, followed by a couple of sentences elaborating on and summarizing each category or heading. Here are the categories in Bonanno and Constance's review (2001, 1):

> The article is divided into four sections. The first provides an overview of the conceptualizations, uses, and critiques of Fordism, post-Fordism, and Globalization as developed in the general economy and society literature. The second section focuses on the conceptualization and use of Fordism in the literature on agriculture and food. The third section presents a review of the recent debate in sociology, rural sociology, political geography, and political economy, highlighting their contribution to macro-level analyses of social change. The final section contains some

concluding remarks about the contributions of this body of literature.

And let's look at it as a numbered list with the items separated by semicolons:

The article is divided into four sections: 1) an overview of the conceptualizations, uses, and critiques of Fordism, post-Fordism, and Globalization as developed in the general economy and society literature; 2) the conceptualization and use of Fordism in the literature on agriculture and food; 3) a review of the recent debate in sociology, rural sociology, political geography, and political economy, highlighting their contribution to macro-level analyses of social change; and 4) concluding remarks about the contributions of this body of literature.

That's it—then you start a new paragraph with the first heading.

Put the focus on the authors in your sentences, but use the right verbs and do not anthropomorphize the research articles. "The researchers wrote," not "The researchers said" and "The authors found," not "The report found."

Now look at an example of a sample student introduction that needs work. The student seems to be writing just to get started. While it becomes apparent after a few sentences that the topic is unequal education, much of the context is missing. What are the actual disparities, and how have they been measured or documented? A reader would first need a brief overview of the history of the educational system in El Salvador (recall from Chapter 1 that context and history are core values of anthropological writing).

There have been studies done on the disparities between urban and rural educational opportunities, yet not as many, it seems, linking gender roles to the problem of unequal education. Reports show the disparity between incomes and education as well as the urban and rural disparities, such as Guzman's report in 2000. The amount of government resources needed to improve education in the rural areas is not available, as "the number of teachers and schools provided for rural areas was seriously inadequate . . . only 15 percent of the nation's school teachers served in rural areas" (Haggarty, 1988). The issue of the difference between women and men's education is touched upon briefly by Guzman when he wrote, "with regard to differences by sex, the educational situation of women appears to be unfavorable when the total population is considered" (Guzman, 2000). Yet he seems to believe that the situation has equaled out in recent years and that girls and boys ages 6–9 have little disparity in attendance at school. There should be further research on what happens later in education during the pre-teen and teen years when children become more responsible for chores at home.

← "There have been studies done" is a weak start to the beginning of the literature review. The first sentence should introduce the topic so that the reader understands what the issues are.

← At this point, it looks like Guzman (2000) is either the seminal work on this topic or the *only* research conducted on this topic. Either way, the student should point this out in a way that shows the student's strengths as a researcher.

Guzman has found that the four most common reasons for El Salvadorians not to study are "'high cost' (lack of economic resources), 'need to go to work,' 'household reasons' and 'not worth the trouble'" (Guzman, 2000). Two of these reasons fit exactly into my research about rural gender perceptions and how that affects schooling. I hope to further this research in looking at how expectations at home for both teen boys and girls affect how seriously they take school and how long they stay in school. Guzman also points out that in a survey taken in 1997, "28% [of those under the age

← It is not immediately clear what kind of organization this lit review is following. The topic is based on El Salvador, but the first paragraph doesn't mention this.

← The student is doing too much direct quoting of sources. The default should be paraphrasing, with sparing use of direct quotation.

of 19] said that the young people concerned did not study because they had to work (including domestic work)." Studies from the 1970s and 80's showed that "there was a high attrition rate in school attendance in rural areas as students left school to earn incomes or work at home" (Haggarty, 1988). These findings were taken in the late 1980's, and it is not known if the situation has improved in rural communities. This issue of domestic work versus schoolwork can have important impacts on how the population of rural El Salvadorians get educated and exceed their parents' generation in years of education.

> ← Good move: The student points out that the research is in need of being updated or repeated.

## Three Ways to Organize the Body

Based on the trends you identified, you can arrange your discussion of the literature in several ways[2]. You might see any of these (or a hybrid of more than one style) used in a literature review, which makes this kind of assignment more creative than you might have originally assumed. Yes, you are using secondary sources that you found through research, but *you* control the arrangement, and that arrangement should be deliberate.

The worst (but unfortunately quite typical) arrangement students adopt tends to go something like this: *Here's one article, which says this; here's another article, which says this; here's another article, which says this.* And so on until they meet the minimum number of sources required. The review then concludes with a dutiful but empty variation on this: *All these articles are on the topic I have been researching.* This kind of *here's one and here's another* organization—or similar arrangements like sequencing sources alphabetically—say to your reader, "I may be able to find and summarize the requisite number of sources, but I can't connect, analyze, or synthesize them."

Such novice literature reviews read like a series of mini-book reports—and that it *not* good because the purpose of a literature review is not simply to prove you did a fair amount of research and reading but instead to show that you see the *relationships* among the sources, that you can make discerning *judgments*, that you can make *connections*, that you can draw *conclusions*.

Here are three more deliberate and logical options for organizing the body:

**By Subtopics**
Arrange your discussion of the literature so that each subtopic is represented by a section heading and described over several paragraphs. Remember to start with the *most important* or *overarching* topic, and then work down in importance. This is the most common form of literature review organization.

**By Chronology**
Sequence from the oldest to the most recent study. If you opt for this, be sure to announce why you are doing it in your introduction. For example, if tracing the development of an idea over time is important, this organization might make the most sense.

**By Population Studied**
If you are conducting a cross-cultural review, this format allows you to describe subpopulations and order them by who

You might also combine organizational styles. For example, you could make your main arrangement by subtopic sections, but then arrange sources within each subtopic section chronologically.

## Tips for Headings

*Make them brief but specific.* Most headings in anthropology reviews are in the range of three to eight words.

Use your key words not only in your title but also in your headings.

*As much as possible, make headings parallel in syntax.* See the *When possible, make elements parallel* section of Chapter 6 if you do not know what this means.

was studied: All age groups/different age groups? Different ethnic groups? Sexes/gender identities? Geographic locations? Situations and/or conditions?

Whatever you choose, choose deliberately.

## Checklist for Assessing Synthesis (or a Lack of It) in Your Sections

- Under each heading, be sure to discuss more than one source.
- In most paragraphs, discuss more than one source. A clue that you are going about this in the wrong way is if you have separate paragraphs for each source. Instead, most of your paragraphs should begin with a point *you* want to make—a statement about an issue, question, claim, method, limitation, counter-argument—and then discuss the relevant sources in relation to that point. That's the synthesis your readers need.
- Several of your individual sentences should include a discussion of more than one source. Again, this shows that you are getting beyond the *here's one source; here's*

> *another source* mode of thinking and instead are per-
> forming synthesis.
> - Some of your sources should be discussed more
>   than once in your review. An important source may
>   be relevant for more than one issue in more than one
>   section. Don't be afraid to circle back to a source you
>   described earlier (so long as it is relevant)—this is a
>   sign not of repetition but of synthesis.

## The Conclusion

Literature reviews should not just stop—they should conclude. Some students resort to summarizing what they have
done earlier, but there are more sophisticated and effective
ways to bring your literature review to a close.

| Tasks to Complete, Questions to Answer | You Write |
| --- | --- |
| Why is this literature review important? | Here is where you explain the "so what" of your literature review. Identify the handful of main points you want the reader to understand. Do not be afraid to number them or use "first, second, third" to guide the reader from one point to the next. |
| If you identified major debates and trends, explain their importance. | "This debate is important because . . ." |
| What are the unanswered questions uncovered by the review? | "Researchers/anthropologists may still not know . . ." |

In your conclusion, incorporate some of the same wording and terms from the introduction (this is called *matching*). The best literature reviews synthesize the existing research around a central question and identify the themes that unite the different works. Remember, the literature review should be an expression of how you are approaching sources, so this section should not just reaffirm that you did the reading but instead should be a place where you reaffirm the more significant *relationships* among the sources and their *implications* for any continuing conversations on your chosen topic.

# WRITING RESEARCH PAPERS

## 5

I'd been slumped with my head in my hands trying to craft a particularly difficult sentence or two for a journal article with a deadline looming. It must have looked like emotional breakdown, but I'd only been caught in the act of writing . . . Some teachers take a very pragmatic, modernist, approach to research: gather your data, order your data, present your data, explain your data. The world is not like that, and nor is human thought. You cannot know what you think until you have put it into words. Writing is thinking in the same way as thrashing your arms around is swimming. One is the material expression of the other. Sometimes, on blissful days, it rattles along. Mostly it doesn't.

—Patrick Sullivan, Associate Professor, Nulungu Research Institute, University of Notre Dame, Australia

Each subfield of anthropology has a preferred style of reporting research. This chapter presents two broad possibilities: the critical research paper and the IMRD (Introduction/Methods/Results/Discussion) report. For cultural anthropologists, the research paper, which tends to read more like an essay than a report, is the main style of communicating original research.

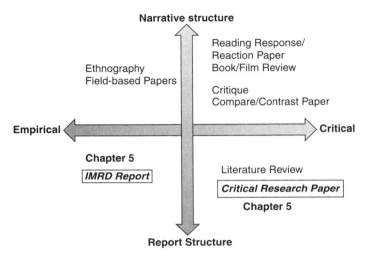

FIGURE 5.1  Structure and Approach for Writing Research Papers.

It falls in the lower right quadrant of the diagram, tending toward *critical* and *report form*. This is addressed in the first part of this chapter.

Meanwhile, archaeologists and biological anthropologists more typically use the IMRD structure, which may be familiar to you from lab reports and research articles in the sciences. This falls in the left lower quadrant and tends to be more *empirical*—that is, to feature original data collected by the writer/researcher. If you are being asked to write in the IMRD format, you will want to turn your attention to the second major section of this chapter.

Medical anthropologists and others who straddle more than one subdiscipline use both formats, depending on the nature of the audience and the publication outlet. If you envision yourself working as part of a multidisciplinary team, you will need to master the IMRD format to maximize the potential number of places to publish.

Both genres involve reviewing the available literature. That is, they depend a great deal on what was covered in Chapter 4 because a literature review is *part* of both genres; it might even constitute *most* of the critical research paper. Given that, make sure you either review Chapter 4 or refer back to it often as you engage with this chapter.

## The Critical Research Paper

The research paper is an essay requiring a thesis statement, argument, and research. For professionals, that research typically involves primary sources (in the form of their own original data, fieldnotes, and such) as well as secondary sources (that is, published books and journal articles). For students, "research" usually involves calling on just those secondary sources, but somehow doing something original with them. Professors typically assign the research paper not only because it approximates the signature genre of anthropology—the journal article—but also because they want you to *develop* your research and critical thinking skills.

Students tend to think that being critical means "identify all the major and nit-picky problems with someone's writing and tear it to shreds." But "be critical" doesn't just mean "be negative," just as "build an argument" doesn't mean "be argumentative." Building upon what was explained in Chapter 1 as developing *critical distance*, here is an elaboration on the power of critical thinking. Critical thinking means being skeptical—that is, not simply accepting information as fact and pushing beyond summary into synthesis, analysis, and argument. Using the Toulmin method of logic (Toulmin 1958, Weida and Stolley 2014), here are some terms to make sure you understand:

- **Claim**: The overall thesis the writer will argue for
- **Data**: Evidence gathered to support the claim

- **Warrant** (also referred to as a bridge): Explanation of why or how the data supports the claim; the underlying assumption that connects your data to your claim
- **Backing** (also referred to as the foundation): Additional logic or reasoning that may be necessary to support the warrant
- **Counterclaim**: A claim that negates or disagrees with the thesis/claim
- **Rebuttal**: Evidence that negates or disagrees with the counterclaim.

One of the most important parts is the warrant, an underlying and often unstated assumption that a writer uses to convince the reader of the argument. Claims must have warrants (Williams 2000). The warrant is the way to understand the writer's agenda. The warrant makes the entire thesis *seem* plausible, and without further scrutiny, incorrect (and potentially dangerous) arguments can be made. When confronted with an argument, the briefest question to ask is, "How do you know?"

In *Anthropology and Human Movement: Searching for Origins*, Drid Williams (2000) identifies other important questions to ask of an argument:

1. What are the claims made by the author?
2. What evidence does the author provide in support of those claims?
3. What warrant(s) subsist "behind" the claims and their supports?

Often writers incorrectly assume that the audience shares the same beliefs, experiences, and point of view. With a faulty warrant, the writer assumes that the reader already agrees, and this may not be true. When the warrant is faulty, the argument may fall apart. This reminds us why some of those basic expectations for anthropological writing covered in Chapter 1—critical distance, engagement, reflexivity, cultural relativism, context/ history, and description—remain important even when your writing relies heavily on sources, as most critical research papers do. Those basic expectations may not constitute the specific warrant behind your own argument, but they usually feed into it—they form the substrate of what readers assume as common knowledge.

The trick to developing your own argument is to first practice identifying claims and warrants in published writing. Then, direct your attention to your claim and evidence: Select and interpret evidence that supports your thesis and arrange it in a compelling and logical order. Based on the data you have, can you confidently make your claim? For all of this to work, you need, of course, to be knowledgeable about your topic. What are the warrants behind your claim?

Critical research papers invite you to come to your own conclusions, to take a stand, and to say something original (or at least synthesize sources in an original way). They usually ask you to use secondary sources—engage with them, interpret them, *challenge* them, as if you are having a conversation with other writers, researchers, and philosophers as relative equals.

## Formulating a Working Thesis

The thesis is actually the *conclusion* that your paper aims to make (Johnson Jr., Rettig, Scott, and Garrison 2004). Students often feel that they have to be fully committed to a thesis statement before they begin writing and that, once set, they're locked into it. Not true. At the outset, your thesis should be a *working* thesis, something that communicates your current main idea but is open to change. Students (and professional researchers!) often find that as they do the research and learn more, they question and adapt their original claims; likewise, as they write, they stumble upon new ideas or counterarguments they did not expect, so they need to adapt. This is healthy. Indeed, one sign of a mature researcher is a willingness to treat research and writing as *processes* of inquiry rather than to decide on a thesis early on and wedge in research to fit it no matter what.

For anthropology papers, the thesis statement must be *debatable*, something that is not a fact or not so commonsensical to your audience that there is little room for debate. To be debatable, a thesis statement should provide new information or a new clarification and contain an element of risk or "tension," as Ramage and Bean (2000) describe it: You have to put yourself out there, be a little provocative or controversial. For example, you could show that a prevailing viewpoint is flawed or incomplete. If your thesis is too rigid or just states what is actually a fact—or is something that anthropologists take as common knowledge (such as "values are relative to culture")—you have nowhere to go, nothing to argue. It is *through* the debate that a reader can see clearly what the specific question is that needs to be answered, the problem that could be solved, or the inquiry that deserves to be pursued. With your thesis, you can be *right* (in the sense that others cannot reasonably disagree with you) and still have a poor thesis because your claim is not debatable.

## More Tips for Constructing an Effective Thesis Statement

- Consider building a counterstatement *into* your thesis; this will give it some productive tension. Many thesis statements contain "although," "while," "but," and "however" to signal that tension. For example, consider these theses: "While Constance argues/suggests . . ., she doesn't account for how . . .," "While most think X on this topic, I will argue Y . . .," or "While most people think X of this culture, I will show . . ." Notice how each of those statements features a *tension* between two things. Not every thesis needs to take this form, but experiment with recrafting yours into one that posits a similar tension.

- A sophisticated move for a thesis statement is to include a subordinate clause that clues readers into the *methods* you will use (or have used) in your paper. Some examples: "<u>Relying on a review of the literature</u>, I argue . . .," "<u>Based on surveys conducted with students at our university</u>, I reveal that . . .," "Drawing on both my own observations of X and a review of the literature . . .," and "By connecting what I have learned in political science on X with a review of several ethnographies on that same topic, I posit that . . ."

- Often good theses include hedging language. Rarely do we *prove* anything in anthropology, so avoid that word. Instead, you interpret, analyze, argue, etc. And sometimes you will want to soften your verbs by saying, "The evidence <u>suggests</u> that . . .," "I will <u>explore</u> how/why . . .," or "In this paper I <u>question</u> the prevailing theory of . . ." Such hedges do not make your thesis *weak*; instead, they usually make you sound *thoughtful*, *measured*, and *realistic*. An overly assertive thesis can make you come across as immature or blind to the complexities of your topic.

At the same time, just as a thesis can't be a restatement of fact or common knowledge in the discipline, it likewise can't be just an opinion. It requires real evidence and reason. So finding the sweet spot is the challenge. The student thesis statements below come from essays on the ethnography *Romance on a Global Stage* (Constable 2003), which is about international marriages started online, and can show you how to discern that sweet spot.

> *Example #1*: "Constable changed the current of popular perspectives on researching transnational marriages, and by doing so she provided the missing voice of the involved individuals."

This statement is not really debatable. The student needs to add some risk. Perhaps the debate could be over what he or she thinks the "missing voice" of the individuals is saying, and whether or not Constable gets their message correct.

> *Example #2*: "In the United States, the term 'mail-order brides' and 'mail-order marriages' have taken on many negative meanings in reference to Asian women. The following will look at how Nicole Constable researched and documented many studies in terms of 'mail-order brides' and 'mail-order marriages' to shed light on how and why Constable feels that the negative meaning of 'mail-order marriage' is unfitting."

The substance is the part about the "how and why" Constable considers the term "mail-order marriage" unfitting, but rather than leave the reader in suspense about why Constable doesn't like the "mail-order marriage" term, the student could answer in the thesis statement the very question he poses and then develop the statement around why his answer is accurate. An alternative could be:

> The following will look at how Nicole Constable researched and documented many studies in terms of "mail-order brides" and "mail-order marriages" to illustrate that Constable considers the term "mail-order marriage" denigrating to couples and perpetuating unequal power dynamics between men and women.
>
> *Example #3*: "Constable's main purpose for writing this book was to defy some of the stereotypes that a lot of people have about 'mail order brides.' She wanted to and did prove that true love can be found through emails and letters. She proves that these online relationships are just like any other—they take work, understanding, commitment and trust."

There is no thesis statement because there's no tension here. Also, "prove" should almost never be in a thesis statement. On questions of interpretation, we rarely prove anything—instead we *persuade* readers of our points of view.

> *Example #4*: "Constable, with her perspective as a feminist, tries through her research to elaborate on the term 'mail-order bride' but doesn't fully liberate the major players involved."

This statement is good because it provides new information (the author is a feminist) and is provocative (by stating that the author doesn't go far enough in achieving her book's goal).

*Example #5:* "The idea of 'mail order brides' is arguably one of the most quickly judged and stereotyped that Constable approaches, as the Westernized view of 'foreign' brides is that they are oppressed, victimized, and thus forced into these situations because of their desperation to escape poverty and 'marry up,' but the reality, as Constable shows, is that these misconceptions are rarely the case."

This one is good because it is detailed and clarifies Constable's view (that these brides are oppressed, victimized, and thus forced into these situations) but also moves the author's idea into a new frame by showing that Constable is correct and what the significance of this is (that Westerners' stereotypes about "mail order brides" are skewed and extreme). It also shows that in your thesis, you need not always disagree with your source— you can also agree and extend his or her thinking.

## Characteristics of a Strong Working Thesis

- Someone could disagree with the statement. (That's good! Then you use evidence and logic to shape your reasoning for why the statement is accurate.)
- Your thesis is focused. Too broad, and it is as if you are trying to cover too much information. Limit your thesis statement; that gives you an opportunity to contribute a new thought or new perspective on the topic.
- Your thesis should not include empty adjectives like *good/bad, appropriate,* or *interesting*; they typically do not add much to the statement and do not make the statement instantly debatable. If you find these words in your working statement, move beyond them to ask

"Why is it good? Why is it interesting?" The response could become a much more provocative thesis.

- Your thesis should answer the "so what?" question. As anthropologist, you must connect a focused thesis to broader human problems.
- Even after these revisions, your thesis must still comport with the original assignment. Designing a great thesis statement is great, but even as you revise it, keep in mind the limits of the original assignment. You may even want to incorporate a key word or two from the assignment into your thesis.

## Composing a Strong Introduction

To write an effective introduction, remember that anthropologists are interested in understanding how your research sheds new light on a relevant anthropological issue, problem, or concept. The introductory section usually contains several paragraphs to provide the context for the time period, geography, people, and issue being studied. It also typically demonstrates a familiarity with secondary sources that are essential to setting the background, which is why typically you should cite one or more sources as part of the introduction.

The introductory section can be summarized as **five** moves:

### 1. *Announce the Topic and Explain Its Significance* (What is the topic?)

Here is where you start to provide background information. To get started, take the key words associated with your topic and start crafting sentences with them. Or consider starting with a definition (not from a dictionary, but from the literature you will cite). Be careful not to start too broadly with statements about "the beginning of time" (see more on this in Chapter 6 in the section *Writing About Time*).

**2. *Provide an Overview of Prior Research* (What do we know?)**
Any seminal works that are directly related to the topic should be mentioned here:

> Ethnographic studies show that participation in clinical trials is mediated by the relationship built between the research community and communities of potential research participants (Graber 2001).

**3. *Include a Statement of the Problem* (What do we not know?)**
Here is where you identify missing information, gaps in scientific knowledge, or the needs that research should fill. It doesn't mean that you should verbally attack the literature. Some options: Note the different limitations of each work; group together several studies, addressing the same limitation for all; or show conflicting findings across several studies. You could refer to multiple studies, noting the different limitations of each:

> Tran and Weiss (1999) attempted to mathematically model the impacts of agriculture on population growth, but their sample size was too small. Gibson-Ganesan (2004) also studied this topic but used only one region in their analysis. A study by DiPaola et al. (2012) used radiocarbon dating to show that early farming societies in Asia grew at the same rate as contemporaneous foraging societies in North America but did not focus on periods later than the Holocene.

You could refer to multiple studies, addressing the same limitation for all:

> Less attention has been paid, however, to the violence perpetrated by women on others. There is still not enough

research on violence against women, but gender differences in the type of violence, incidence rates, and victimization need further scrutiny (Clim and Johnson 2014; Winn 2013).

You could refer to multiple studies, showing conflicting findings:

However, the evidence on effectiveness of needle exchange programs is controversial. Some studies find that needle exchange patients have a greater baseline severity of drug use than patients in the standard referral group (Rooney et al. 2016; Brothers et al. 2014), which might affect success rates, while others find that the true issue with needle exchange programs may not be the success rate at all but the problem of "NIMBY" (not in my backyard) public and legislative opposition (Campbell 2013). Evaluation of needle exchange programs suffers from a lack of similar measures, which contributes to these mixed findings . . .

### 4. *Explain the Contribution of Your Research* (What does this research add to what we know?)
Here is where you start to pivot toward your own research. You might spend those initial paragraphs building your argument, but the last paragraph of the introductory section before the first of the customized headings is where you really reinforce it:

I examine . . .
I argue . . .
I investigate . . .
I suggest . . .

In this article I apply the use of myths about transgender people to understand American lawmakers' assumptions about American society and gender norms. I argue that the protection of children is being used as a fulcrum to attract public support for bills that would negatively affect not only transgender individuals but also individuals who are not gender nonconforming. Survey research on gender beliefs needs further development in order to capture the quickly changing public opinion on transgender people. I present recent research on attitudes toward transgender people as a potential avenue into understanding contemporary gender attitudes, using it to illustrate the challenges of . . .

### 5. *Describe the Methods Used* (**What are the** *how, where,* **and** *when* **of this study?**)

In research papers for anthropology, the methods section is usually a paragraph combined with the other introductory paragraphs. If you attend enough anthropology conferences, you might hear in the hallways some audience members mumbling about how the speaker they just heard did not describe his or her methods in detail or even at all. When you downplay the methods, even for the purposes of a brief presentation, the audience becomes skeptical. Providing details about methods is part of being a scientist. Here's an example of the final introductory paragraph of "History's remainders: on time and objects after conflict in Cyprus" by Rebecca Bryant (2014) in *American Ethnologist*:

..................................................................................................................................

The conflict context, then, makes clear the role of the future in finding a home in history, emphasizing the future as a dimension of the living present, a present that is always in the process of making the past. In the argument that follows, I use long-term    ← The first sentence provides background and suggests a gap or need for research.

fieldwork in Cyprus to show how and why objects may be used to work through histories that are contested and anxiously viewed as incomplete. I argue (1) that objects contain a temporal dynamism that points them in uncertain ways toward the future. In the particular context of the border opening, the capacity of houses, wardrobes, and photographs to emit or evoke multiple possible futures created anxiety that is overcome through use of such objects for historical work. Such historical work depends (2) on the conjoining of persons and things through the polyvalent concept of "belonging," which people use to describe relationships of care, interdependence, and right. I describe a context in which the "belongness" of belongings is contested and in which (3) the claims of belonging are made by reworking relations of past, present, and future. Practices with and stories about belongings, then, may also help us to "belong" in history.

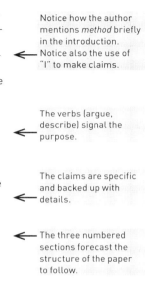

Notice how the author mentions *method* briefly in the introduction. Notice also the use of "I" to make claims.

The verbs (argue, describe) signal the purpose.

The claims are specific and backed up with details.

The three numbered sections forecast the structure of the paper to follow.

It might surprise scientists who expect a detailed methods section that "long-term fieldwork" is the only mention in this paper of any methods used in the collection of the findings. But in this format, the emphasis is on the richness of the data, which is used in conjunction with additional historical context and quotations from informants. The reader must rely on the anthropologist's voice and knowledge of the subject to make appropriate interpretations of the data.

Using Anita Hannig's (2015) research article "Sick healers: chronic affliction and the authority of experience at an Ethiopian hospital," we can see each of the five moves. The bolded parts signal the moves and the transition from one to the next.

The anthropological and therapeutic record abounds with examples of the virtues of experiential expertise—that is, the idea that a person's subjective illness experience can bolster her credentials for assisting others, similarly afflicted, in moving from a state of disease to well-being. Victor Turner's (1967) classic account of the Ndembu ritual adept who advances from patient to healer comes to mind, as do other accounts of so-called "wounded healers" (Devisch 1993; Halifax 1979; Moore et al. 1999; Taussig 1987). In a somewhat-analogous fashion, contemporary treatment programs for HIV/AIDS and Ebola have made use of so-called "expert patients"—lay medical workers whose own health has improved through treatment and who now aid in the therapeutic journey of others (Kyakuwa et al. 2012; Schneider et al. 2006). Yet, just as personal illness experience can imbue the figure of the healer—broadly construed—with special authority, it can also have a profoundly delegitimizing effect. In the hospital in Ethiopia that I studied, uncured patients who had been hired as nurse assistants hid their medical histories from their patients for fear that patients would reject treatment from them, especially injections. Even though these women considered their own experiences as patients as great assets in offering care, a disclosure of this experience risked undermining their medical authority on the ward.

In this article, I embark on an ethnographic and analytic exploration of healing authority inside an Ethiopian fistula hospital. Attending to the example of these Ethiopian nurse–patients can yield fresh insights into the construction of biomedical authority in global clinical settings and illuminate an understudied dimension of what it means to

*Move 1: Announces the topic (patient experiences) and situates it as a common topic in medical anthropology.*

*Move 2: Previous research is summarized. Note citation use.*

*Move 3: This research is going to look at the phenomenon of how patients might feel delegitimized when they themselves become lay healers for others.*

*Move 4: This research contributes to the knowledge of how authority is constructed for lay healers in a biomedical environment.*

suffer from chronic illness. With the exception of studies on medical socialization (Good and Good 1993; Lief and Fox 1963; Wendland 2010) and a few recent hospital-based ethnographies (Livingston 2012; Street 2014), medical anthropologists have focused most of their attention on the lives and histories of those who receive care, not on those who provide it inside clinical settings. Similarly, the literature on chronic illness has been largely patient centered, with the figure of the patient being someone other than the practitioner (Estroff 1993; Garcia 2010; Jackson 2005; Manderson and Smith-Morris 2010). Far less attention has been paid to those whose medical condition implicates them as both care receivers and caregivers in contemporary healing therapeutics. In this article, I add a new perspective to the study of chronicity by examining how the chronic afflictions of caregivers may influence daily clinical dynamics.

← Back to Moves 2 and 3, to point out a group of studies with the same limitation *and* identify the gap that this research will fill: understanding of nurse-patients as caregivers.

I spent the year of 2010 and previous summers conducting ethnographic research on the bodily, religious, and social dimensions of obstetric fistula and its treatment in two clinical settings in Ethiopia. Obstetric fistula is a maternal childbirth injury that results from prolonged, obstructed labor that is unrelieved by an emergency medical intervention, such as a Caesarean section. The protracted pressure of the stuck fetus against the mother's pelvic tissues produces a hole in her bladder and sometimes her rectum wall, rendering her incontinent of urine or feces, and sometimes both. The baby almost never survives the multi-day ordeal of labor. Whereas obstetric fistula is extremely rare in resource-rich countries, it affects an estimated two million women in the Global South, most of whom live in Sub-Saharan Africa. At specialized fistula hospitals all across Ethiopia, which are run under the

← Move 5: The writer announces her methods, which involve ethnographic research conducted in Ethiopia.

umbrella of the NGO Hamlin Fistula International, women can access free surgery to attempt to repair these injuries and regain their continence. I carried out the majority of my research at the regional fistula repair center in Bahir Dar, the capital of the northwestern Amhara region of Ethiopia.

## CHECKLIST FOR WRITING INTRODUCTIONS

✓ Does the introduction clearly announce the topic and explain its significance? The introduction should begin by introducing the topic briefly, perhaps with definitions from the literature in a way that is clear enough that readers unfamiliar with it can grasp the general area of this research. Is the topic question or problem oriented?

✓ Does the introduction clearly provide an overview of prior research? The introduction should provide a purposeful review of prior, relevant research.

✓ Does the introduction clearly include a statement of the problem? The introduction should clearly identify missing information, gaps in scientific knowledge, or the needs that research should fill.

✓ Does the introduction clearly explain how the present work contributes to previous research? The introduction should state the *kind(s)* of evidence you have collected and explain *how* that evidence makes a meaningful contribution to answering the broader research question. In other words, what do we know now that we did not know before?

✓ Does the introduction clearly signal which move is occurring at each point?

✓ For critical research papers, are the methods appropriately described in the Introduction?

One important thing to remember about your introduction is that it is a roadmap, not a travelog. A short and concise introduction should be the ideal. Resist the impulse to tell your reader everything at this stage. If you are into your third or fourth page and your reader still does not know your research question, go back and rewrite your introduction.

## Filling in the Body

A good working thesis and a strong introduction should telegraph the structure of the paper's body. Unlike with the IMRD paper described later in this chapter, you will need to create customized headings to announce each section. That is, don't use "Introduction," "Body," and "Conclusion" but instead use thematic headings. For example, the article "'This is not a parade, it's a protest march': intertextuality, citation, and political action on the streets of Bolivia and Argentina" used four subsequent headings:

- *Intertextuality, Political Ritual, and Political Action*
- *Political Agency Expressed in Physical Form*
- *(Sensorial) Intertextuality and the Protest Repertoire*
- *Citation, Intertextuality, and the Co-Construction of Meaning.*

Notice that most of the headings echo the key words of the title even as they introduce new key topics for each section.

Because each critical research paper is different, there is no easy formula for how many sections you should have or how long each should be, but in general, papers will include three to five body sections and each will include three to 10 paragraphs. Figures, photos, and other visuals will be woven in to each section as fitting (be sure to label each one).

The bulk of the body will involve reviewing the literature, which means that nearly all of the strategies covered in Chapter 4 will apply here. Therefore, when writing your body, revisit that chapter. If stuck on how to organize your sections, you might

## Introduce Counterarguments

Sometimes, students think that they will weaken their argument if they point out its flaws. In academic writing, just the opposite is true. Sophisticated writers identify contrary points of view (known as counterarguments), describe the other sides of the issue or alternative interpretations of the data (known as concessions), and acknowledge the limitations of their own research. You can do this in the introductory section or any of the body paragraphs. Here's where you use the transitional words described in the *Employ Precision Transitions* part of Chapter 6 to mark places in the paper where you are contradicting another author's idea.

Other options include these:

> *It might [seem/appear/look/etc.] as if . . .* [state the counterargument here].
> *Opposing views include/Other critics claim . . .* [state the counterargument here].

Concessions admit that the counterargument is indeed valid. A typical concession takes the shape of a "It may be true that . . . but" statement where you can end strong with a rebuttal reinforcing your own position: "Nonetheless . . ."

Other options are these:

> *While that may be*
>    *the case that . . .*     *Certainly . . .*
> *Admittedly . . .*         *While it is true that . . .*

find the section *Three Modes of Organizing the Body* particularly helpful, but note that in a critical research paper, your argument, and not just a survey of the literature, should drive the structure.

## Finishing with a Strong Conclusion

Some students think that conclusions are only for restating the thesis and summarizing, but conclusions need to do more. If needed, reuse a key concept that you introduced in the introductory section and quickly recap your main conclusions, but also consider:

- What patterns did you uncover?
- Why do they matter? This is that "so what?" question. (As an exercise to get you thinking in this direction, try filling in this statement: "This argument matters for _____ because _____.")
- Can you connect the argument that you carefully established with the larger, more universal human characteristics in anthropology, such as conflict, morality, family, or distribution of resources?
- What are the implications—practical, intellectual, or ethical— of your argument or your findings?
- Can the kinds of work you have done in the paper be extended to other texts or contexts?
- What is left unanswered? What new questions does the research provoke?

Indeed, in your concluding section or paragraph you can quite literally pose a question or two. But most of all, understand that compelling conclusions do not try to shut down conversation and have the last word (therefore, avoid formulations like, "As you can see, I have incontrovertibly proven that . . .").

Instead, they push to keep the conversation going in light of what you have just argued in your critical research paper.

## The Introduction/Methods/Results/Discussion (IMRD) Report Format

The IMRD report format is the most common structure for presenting completed research in the sciences. While these papers have a formulaic structure, they are difficult to write. You have probably used this format for lab reports in your biology or psychology courses. For anthropology, the structure is no different, except the IMRD format is only one genre—and not necessarily the dominant genre—in which all anthropologists write. Psychology and anthropology share some similarities. The participants are (usually) human and researchers in both fields are interested in what they think and how their research subjects think, act, or behave. Psychologists, however, tend to manipulate the research environment to approximate experimental conditions. Psychologists, unlike anthropologists, sometimes create scenarios to control variables for the purpose of an experiment, and then the participant is debriefed. Rather than manipulate variables or change the environment to fit desired conditions, anthropologists tend to do naturalistic research.

An IMRD research report includes three literature reviews: 1) in the introduction, where you provide the background on the topic and the problem being investigated; 2) in the methods section (this one is very small), where you cite sources that have previously used the methods you used; and 3) in the discussion section, where you provide a review of new knowledge and further connect the findings from the research to other ideas. There are conventions for which verb tenses to use for each section, and you can find those tips in the section of Chapter 6 titled *When to Use Present, Past, and Future Verb Tenses.*

You do not have to write the sections in the IMRD sequence—indeed, few experienced writers compose their introduction first (or they do it very roughly, knowing that they will need to revise it later). Instead, most start by writing the sections that come easiest to them: methods, then results/findings, followed by the discussion, the introduction, and the abstract.

## Methods

The methods section is a good place to start writing a report on original research because it is the easiest to write: You tell the reader what you did and how you did it. Unsuccessful methods sections obscure the procedural details; they lack a series of clear steps, and it is unclear who is doing what. For example, it's not enough for a cultural anthropologist to simply state that he or she conducted "participant observation" without elaborating on the "who, what, where, when," and especially "how" of the procedures that were undertaken in the research. A strong methods section provides a clear picture of the research setting or site, the study population or sampling strategy, and the kinds of questions asked in a survey or interview. If more than one method is being used, each method should clearly attempt to answer a part of a research question. A strong methods section also refers to (and cites) other works whose methods have informed your own. This becomes especially important if you are varying a method; in this section,

Most experienced writers start an IMRD report by composing their methods or results sections. Therefore, in this chapter we start with methods, move on to results and discussion, and only then cover introductions and abstracts. Consider writing your introduction and abstract last.

you must explain what's being modified, how, and why, such as "We employ a variant of the method developed by James (1988) . . ." It is a common mistake to include methods in the results section.

Introduce analyses simply: "The data were analyzed using chi-square." If you have missing data, you should state this in this section. The results and discussions sections can sometimes be combined if the author wants to have a more reader-friendly results section.

As an example of a strong methods section, here are the first sentences from the first paragraph of a three-paragraph methods section from a research article by Boeri, Gibson, and Harbry (2009) describing the ethnographic methods they used in their substance use research:

> In our ethnographic study on methamphetamine use in the suburbs we used qualitative methods that are particularly applicable for studies among hidden populations (Carlson et al., 2004; Lambert, Ashery, & Needle, 1995; Shaw, 2005; Small, Kerr, Charrette, Schechter, & Spittal, 2006). The data collection included: (a) participant observations, (b) drug history and life history matrices, and (c) audio-recorded in-depth interviews. We spent at least 20 h a week over the course of a year in the field to become familiar with the environment of the study population and to develop community contacts (Agar, 1973; Bourgois, 1995; Sterk-Elifson, 1993). A combination of targeted, snowball, and theoretical sampling methods were used to recruit respondents for the study (Strauss & Corbin, 1998; Watters & Biernacki, 1989).

It is clear, even from this brief excerpt, that the authors are confident ethnographers who detail exactly what methods they employed to answer their research question, which they summarized in the first words of the first sentence.

The methods section describes the sample size and strategy for how you obtained your participants, how they were recruited, and any methods or instruments/measures used for collecting data. This section also describes any statistical analyses used on the data. Do not gloss over *how* you analyzed the data; instead describe the procedures in as much detail as you can. If you used any special analytical software, mention it. (Note that not all anthropologists believe software should be used in qualitative research; software should be a tool used to facilitate the anthropologist's own analysis, not to replace it.) For qualitative analysis, walk the reader through the process of how you approached the data. Did you read and reread interview transcripts? Did you develop a codebook and look for patterns that fit those codes in the interviews?

## Results

The first one or two paragraphs of a results section summarize the data, such as the participants' demographic characteristics, what the instruments measured, responses to questionnaires described as percentages, or multivariate analyses. Much of the analyses end up becoming intermediate steps on the way to a clearer answer to a research question, so you will not be able to put all your data and all the calculations into the results section.

For a qualitative project, figuring out what to put in this section is more difficult. A helpful table is the Consolidated Criteria for Reporting Qualitative studies (COREQ), a 32-item checklist that provides "best practices" for what to include in a qualitative research report based on interviews and/or focus groups (Tong, Sainsbury, and Craig 2007). This checklist is designed for healthcare providers writing up interview and healthcare data for publication and is more limited than the full breadth of qualitative research, but it provides some structure and prevents some "oh, I forgot to write about that!" moments.

## Presenting Your Data: Charts, Graphs, or Maps?

You might have used science to analyze your data, but making effective visual representations of your findings is an art. The purpose of figures and tables is to help your reader understand your data. Figures and tables can be time-consuming to produce, but you also know bad ones when you see them:

- Too many lines or colors
- Confusing symbols
- Too many units in a single figure
- Crowded text

Information in tables can be more easily compared while reading down rather than across, so make the columns the dependent variables and the rows the independent variables (Matthews and Matthews 2008). Every visual data representation should have a descriptive title and useful labeling (National Cancer Institute—Office of Communications and Education 2011). Using colors can be very helpful for showing comparisons, but having too many colors is distracting. Do not use red and green together. When they're adjacent to each other, they contrast; also, people with red-green colorblindness will not be able to distinguish between the colors. Pie charts are considered bad graphs because it is difficult to see the differences in size between the slices, so trends can be obscured. In fact, there is a movement in data visualization against pie charts (Marr 2014).

This table describes different kinds of pictures and offers suggestions for making them easily understandable to your reader:

Visual Data

| Representation | Purpose | Do | Do Not |
|---|---|---|---|
| **Tables** | Compare number values | Use shading, bolding, and white spaces | Include more than one value in a cell of a table |
| **Bar charts** | Use height or length to show relative differences | Use as few bars as you need to make your data understood | Overlay lines over bars |
| **Scatterplots** | Show the correlation, the relationship between two variables (the horizontal and vertical axes) with points | Use a trend line to show the general direction of the points | Use colors just to make the graph pretty |
| **Line graphs** | Connect data points into lines to show trends | Put labels as close to the lines on the graphs as possible | Clutter the graph with extra lines |
| **Histogram** | Show the distribution of numerical data | Use meaningful ranges of equal size | Use a histogram to represent categories (use a bar chart) |
| **Maps** | Show frequency over a geographic space | Use colors or shading to show variation | Include too much information on the map |
| **Flow charts** | Describe a process from start to finish | Use consistent shapes and arrows | Make the graph difficult to follow by going from right to left or creating a circular path |

## Discussion

The discussion is all about how you interpret the results you obtained. Here is where you explain what the data *show, demonstrate, support,* or *indicate*. For the discussion, worry about the data you have, not what you do not have. A typical discussion section contains the following information:

- Summary of the findings. You should also restate the research question. By explaining and restating, you are emphasizing what you want readers to remember (Sternberg 1993).
- Strengths of the study
- Limitations of the study, including sources of potential bias, errors in measurement, imprecise instruments/measures. However, don't beat yourself up too much in this section; every study has flaws.
- Generalizability of the findings
- Implications of the study's findings for future research, practice, or policy (Cooper and American Psychological Association 2011).

Don't forget that for a quantitative study where hypotheses were tested, this section is where you should state whether the results support or fail to support your hypothesis.

Rosnow and Rosnow (2012) suggest the following further questions to consider:

- How do the results relate to the purpose?
- Were there any serendipitous findings of interest?
- How valid and generalizable are the findings?
- Are there larger implications in the findings?

- Is there an alternative way to interpret the results?
- Do the results raise new questions?

## The Introduction

The introduction frames the topic of the research and how it fits into broader directions of research. Why is this research being conducted? Why do we need additional information on this topic? Sometimes this is referred to as a "gap" in our scientific knowledge. Science is not necessarily holes to be plugged with new studies; instead, think about what contributions your study can make and how new connections can be made. What would this new information allow us to do next? The introduction consists of at least one, and usually a few, paragraphs that include all or most of the following: the purpose of the study, a statement of the problem, and the research objectives: "The goal of this research is to . . ." or "Our objectives are . . ." Include a description of the research design, sometimes referred to as the "research strategy" or the "approach." If you are applying a specific theory or concept, here is where you explain it and any definitions you intend to use. This is called *operationalization* and involves explaining how a complex phenomenon like climate change can be broken down and measured using variables like vulnerability and resilience, which themselves can be measured using other variables.

Here's the introduction and approach from "Climate challenges, vulnerabilities, and food security" by Nelson and colleagues (2016), which was published in *Proceedings of the National Academy of Sciences* (*PNAS*). Notice that *PNAS* has a convention of not having the first section titled "Introduction." Also notice that concepts not originating from the authors are appropriately attributed to other researchers (for more information on citations, see Chapter 7, "Citing Your Sources"). The text boxes outline the goal of each paragraph.

Managing disasters, especially those that are climate-induced, calls for reducing vulnerabilities as an essential step in reducing impacts (1–8). Exposure to environmental risks is but one component of potential for disasters. Social, political, and economic processes play substantial roles in determining the scale and kind of impacts of hazards (1, 8–12). "Disasters triggered by natural hazards are not solely influenced by the magnitude and frequency of the hazard event (wave height, drought intensity etc.), but are also rather heavily determined by the vulnerability of the affected society and its natural environment" (ref. 1, p. 2). Thus, disaster planning and relief should address vulnerabilities, rather than returning a system to its previous condition following a disaster event (6).

<- Statement of the problem

Using archaeologically and historically documented cultural and climate series from the North Atlantic Islands and the US Southwest, we contribute strength to the increasing emphasis on vulnerability reduction in disaster management. We ask whether there are ways to think about climate uncertainties that can help people build resilience to rare, extreme, and potentially devastating climate events. More specifically, we ask whether vulnerability to food shortfall before a climate challenge predicts the scale of impact of that challenge. Our goal is both to assess current understandings of disaster management and to aid in understanding how people can build the capability to increase food security and reduce their vulnerability to climate challenges.

<- Contributions that this study is making; this study's objectives

We present analyses of cases from substantially different regions and cultural traditions that show strong relationships between levels of vulnerability to food shortage before rare climate events and the impact of those events. The patterns and

<- Argument for (1) the importance of this research and (2) why food security is being studied this way

details of the different contexts support the view that vulnerability cannot be ignored. These cases offer a long-term view rarely included in studies of disaster management or human and cultural well-being (for exceptions, see refs. 13 and 14). This long time frame allows us to witness changes in the context of vulnerabilities and climate challenges, responding to a call for more attention to "how human security changes through time, and particularly the dynamics of vulnerability in the context of multiple processes of change" (ref. 10, p. 17).

## Approach

In this study, we focus on climate challenges that can impact food security, one of the seven human securities identified by a United Nations Human Development Report (15) (see also ref. 10) and one of the core components of human well-being as identified by the Millennium Ecosystem Assessment Board (16). Food security refers to "physical and economic access to basic food" (ref. 15, p. 27). Integral to our perspective is a multidimensional conceptualization of food security as involving both the availability of food and access to that food (e.g., 17, 18). The capability of people to access food can be limited by structural and social conditions (19, 20), as we identify in this study.

⬅ How this study is conceptualized in relation to food security

We use the concept of vulnerability to assess resilience of food security to climate challenges. Resilience is the ability of a system to absorb disturbances without losing its identity (21) and its capacity to absorb perturbations or shocks while maintaining essential structures and functions (22, 23). Vulnerability is "the state of susceptibility to harm from exposure to stresses associated with environmental and social change and from the absence of capacity to adapt" (ref. 24, p. 268). Turner

⬅ Definitions of vulnerability and resilience, in relation to food security and climate changes

and colleagues (9) identify exposure, sensitivity, and resilience as key components of vulnerability. Our study focuses specifically on Turner et al.'s dimension of sensitivity. We examine conditions that impact the capability of people to maintain food security, including both availability and access. Vulnerability to climate challenges is mediated by institutional structures (23) (see also refs. 11 and 25) that are constantly changing and impacting people's capabilities to avoid declines in food security.

Disaster managers are especially concerned ◄── Intended contributions
with vulnerabilities, the preconditions that       of this study
lead climate challenges such as droughts,
floods, and extreme cold conditions to become
disasters, recognizing that it is at the interface
of environmental and social conditions that
disasters occur (9, 12, 13, 26). Our research
builds on arguments that resilience to the
impacts of climate (and other) challenges can
be built by reducing vulnerabilities (2–6, 9, 12).
However, people "tend to push the risk spectrum toward catastrophic events occurring
with increasing probability" (ref. 14, p. 8).

To explore the relationship between vulner-   ◄── Brief forecast of the
ability, food security, and the impacts of cli-       study design
mate challenges, we quantify social and
climate conditions in seven centuries-long
sequences. First, we identify 13 points in our
climate sequences that are rare and extreme.
We then quantify the extent of vulnerability to
food shortfall for the period immediately preceding each climate event. Finally, we identify
the conditions following each climate event in
terms of major social changes and declines
in food security, specifically food shortage.
We compare these conditions with the vulnerability before each climate challenge to consider the role of vulnerabilities in the impact
of climate challenges.

This introductory section is a good example of an IMRD setup because each paragraph has an intended purpose and together they build an argument for not only the scientific basis for the project but also showing the direct path from A to B to C and so on. For additional strategies on composing introductions, flip back to the *Composing a Strong Introduction* section for the critical research paper earlier in this chapter.

## The Abstract

An abstract is a brief summary of any work—a research paper, a book chapter, a conference paper, or a poster. Abstracts are *extremely* important to researchers because a brief yet thorough abstract helps researchers decide on the relevance of your project to *their* research and whether they should include your study in their literature reviews. For experienced researchers, that decision usually takes just seconds, and a good abstract makes it easier for researchers to do their work.

Sometimes, abstract writing is an assignment in itself, where students practice distilling articles into 200- to 300-word summaries. For publications, abstracts could run as few as 150 words, and some conferences call for abstracts of just 100 words.

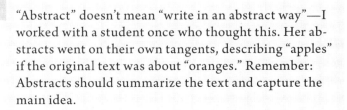

"Abstract" doesn't mean "write in an abstract way"—I worked with a student once who thought this. Her abstracts went on their own tangents, describing "apples" if the original text was about "oranges." Remember: Abstracts should summarize the text and capture the main idea.

A typical abstract contains the following information:

- Statement of the problem that the research study addresses
- Brief but specific information on method, including research design, sample size, measures, and participants (number and type)
- Major findings
- Main implications of the findings and any conclusions (Cooper and American Psychological Association 2011).

In science and the humanities, there are two main types of abstracts, and because anthropology bridges both, anthropologists need to be able to write both.

The first is the *descriptive abstract* (for research papers). It is short, usually 100 to 200 words, and describes the background of the research and the major arguments to be discussed (University of Adelaide Writing Centre 2014). You'll see "I argue" statements and presentation of a theoretical framework, usually to contest or challenge it. This abstract is found primarily in the humanities and social sciences, although psychology tends to adopt a more structured informative abstract style for research reporting.

Here's an example of a descriptive abstract from Ruth E. Toulson's (2014) piece "Eating the food of the gods: interpretive dilemmas in anthropological analysis" in the journal *Anthropology and Humanism*:

> In critical opposition to the pathologizing processes of psychiatric diagnosis, anthropologists have interpreted

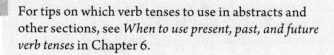

For tips on which verb tenses to use in abstracts and other sections, see *When to use present, past, and future verb tenses* in Chapter 6.

the actions of individuals in psychological pain as forms of resistance. However, I suggest that such analyses often presume rather than trace the connection between the unsettled psyche and social life, in a manner that mirrors the dehumanization of biomedical categorization. In this article I examine events at a temple in Singapore where, in an act others regarded as deeply concerning, a woman climbed over the altar and ate the food left for the gods. My initial analytic strategy was to interpret her actions as a form of taciturn rebellion, as a commentary on the realities of life within a patriarchal family and under an authoritarian state. However, an experience from my own life prompted me to reconsider this reading and to interrogate the ways in which her experience was elided by my original analysis.

Notice that it is not really clear what the specific findings are; the abstract ends in an open-ended way. An advantage to this abstract style is that a reader might be intrigued enough to want to read the entire article; a disadvantage is that a reader probably will need to read the entire article to fully understand the research.

The second type of abstract is an *informative abstract* (for IMRD reports). This abstract's structure leaves little to the imagination. The abstract summarizes the background, the problem, methods, major findings, and any conclusions or recommendations that are described in more detail in the full-length paper. There's no new information here. Depending on the research journal, the abstract might require a very rigid structure as opposed to a paragraph: Introduction, Methods, Results, and Conclusions, with each mini-section starting on a new line.

Here's an abstract on the feeding behaviors of juvenile capuchin monkeys for the article "Age-related variation in the mechanical properties of foods processed by Sapajus libidinosus" (Chalk et al. 2016) in the *American Journal of Physical Anthropology*:

*Abstract*

Objectives: The diet of tufted capuchins (Sapajus) is characterized by annual or seasonal incorporation of mechanically protected foods. Reliance on these foods raises questions about the dietary strategies of young individuals that lack strength and experience to access these resources. Previous research has demonstrated differences between the feeding competencies of adult and juvenile tufted capuchins. Here we test the hypothesis that, compared to adults, juveniles will process foods with lower toughness and elastic moduli.

Materials and Methods: We present data on variation in the toughness and elastic modulus of food tissues processed by Sapajus libidinosus during the dry season at Fazenda Boa Vista, Brazil. Food mechanical property data were collected using a portable universal mechanical tester.

Results: Results show that food tissues processed by the capuchins showed significant differences in toughness and stiffness. However, we found no relationship between an individual's age and mean or maximum food toughness or elastic modulus, indicating both juvenile and adult S. libidinosus are able to process foods of comparable properties.

Discussion: Although it has been suggested that juveniles avoid mechanically protected foods, age-related differences in feeding competence are not solely due to variation in food toughness or stiffness. Other factors related to food type (e.g., learning complex behavioral sequences, achieving manual dexterity, obtaining physical strength to lift stone tools, or recognizing subtle cues about food state) combined with food mechanical properties better explain variation in juvenile feeding competency.

Although the abstract is read first, it is written last when it is a part of a longer document like a proposal or report. Professional writers want either the broadest, largest readership possible or the most appropriate readership, depending on the intended audience. The abstract should be readable in plain English and should contain only the essential technical terms. Adding too many technical terms or acronyms risks sounding like jargon, but including some technical terms allows readers who are familiar with those terms to more quickly grasp the main ideas of your research. It also allows search engines and other indexing systems to pull up your research when others are searching using technical terms. Using search engine optimization, you can try to make your study as high on the results list as possible (Berrett 2016).

So when editing the final version of your abstract, think backwards: How would a researcher search for a paper like yours? What search terms would he or she use? For example, if your study is about the gender-based structure of Mayan families, you would want to include the following key terms in your title and abstract:

- family structure (as a phrase)
- kin, kinship
- Mayan
- Guatemala
- gender

It seems as if abstracts should be easy to write, but most writers need to revise them across several drafts. If you are struggling to get your abstract under the required word limit, you may find strategies in the *Be Concise* section of Chapter 6 particularly helpful.

# EDITING FOR STYLE

## 6

> I think of myself as a writer who happens to be doing his
> writing as an anthropologist.
>
> —Clifford Geertz

Writing is difficult for nearly everyone, but typically you only see the shiny finished product, not the messy drafts that preceded it. Most academic writing—even the writing your professors do—goes through at least three stages (and often many more): a first draft where the ideas are formed and the structure begins to take shape; a second where large chunks of text are added, cut, and moved around; and a third focused on striving for just the right wording, cutting any extraneous verbiage, refining transitions, and checking for correct grammar, punctuation and source citation (Smyth 2004). This chapter is about that third stage (although we'll defer issues related to citing sources until the next chapter).

Anthropologists want to see a certain style in their students' writing but might have trouble explaining what that looks like or how to achieve it. That can leave us with instruction akin to Chief Justice Potter's 1964 threshold test of pornography for the Supreme Court: "I know it when I see it." That kind of response, however, is not really instruction at all, but this chapter is: You'll see what to look for and learn what to do.

Sentence-level editing certainly involves fixing common grammar and usage problems, but I hope that you'll come to see that it is about more than just correcting. Editing for clarity is about being considerate of your readers—taking care to think of *their* needs and not make them muddle through tangled prose—and showing readers that you care enough about your *own* work to present it in a professional way.

Style also carries discipline-specific consequences. It involves following conventions that anthropologists as a community have come to adopt, many of which are informed by core intellectual and ethical values in the discipline. In this sense, hewing close to stylistic norms shows that you understand and accept those values—that you are an insider.

At the same time, there is enormous variety in anthropological writing, and style can (and should) also be about finding your own voice, marking your individuality, albeit within reasonable disciplinary boundaries. This chapter will not emphasize individuality much, but over the long term you should think about developing your writerly voice, and one way to do that is to read widely in the field and imitate the stylistic moves of anthropologists whose work you come to admire. The push toward convention, the pull toward individuality: That is the hard work of editing for style.

## Race, Ethnicity, and Special Populations

Anthropologists are acutely aware of issues of race, such as the presence of racial bias in science, or how descriptors for race and ethnicity are often used interchangeably (and imprecisely). In the 1990s the American Anthropological Association (AAA) issued specific statements that object to framing race as determined by phenotype (http://www.aaanet.org/stmts/racepp.htm) and to framing intelligence as biologically determined by race (http://www.aaanet.org/stmts/race.htm).

If you write about race, you should make it clear from the outset that you understand the argument that race is a social construct, not a biological fact. Some scholars set off race in quotation marks, as Mukhopadhyay and Moses (1997) do in the title of their article, "Reestablishing 'Race' in Anthropological Discourse," while others use the phrase *social race* as a signifier of the social interpretations of race. When writing about ethnicity, be aware of its strong ties to identity, history, language, migration, nation-building, and ethnic conflict.

Use the emic terms—that is, the terms that ethnic groups use to describe themselves—and not the terms that their adversaries call them. For example, "Anasazi" is a word originating from the Diné (Navajo People) to describe the Pueblo people as "ancient enemies." Even though you might see "Anasazi" in older documents, you should use "Ancestral Puebloans" instead (National Park Service 2016). Not all authors accept these changes easily. David Roberts, who is not an anthropologist, "grudgingly" uses the term "Ancestral Puebloans" in his writing and considers the change a turn toward political correctness since, he argues, no one knows the name that the Ancestral Puebloans used to call themselves (Roberts 2015).

When writing about ethnic groups, be as precise as possible. For example, if you are writing about Dominicans, use that specific descriptor rather than "Hispanics," a U.S. term that encompasses Latin American or Spanish people of any ethnicity or race, or "Latinos," a term that in the United States denotes people with ties to Latin America (U.S. Census Bureau 2013). Likewise, the phrase "the Chinese" risks being an overly broad generalization. Is this phrase referring to all Chinese people? As a nationality or a cultural group? One way to be more precise is to cut the definite article "the" and instead use "Chinese" as an adjective, as in "Chinese participants" or "Chinese-American children who were part of the study."

You can find good guidelines for writing about race and ethnicity in an unusual place: medical journals. The medical periodical *Journal of the American Medical Association (JAMA) Internal Medicine* (JAMA Internal Medicine 2016) dictates these guidelines for summarizing the racial and ethnic backgrounds of research participants:

> If race and/or ethnicity is reported, indicate in the "Methods" section who classified individuals as to race/ethnicity, the classifications, and whether the options were defined by the investigator or the participant. Explain why race and/or ethnicity was assessed in the study.
>
> For studies involving humans categorized by race/ethnicity, age, disease/disabilities, religion, sex/gender, sexual orientation, or other socially constructed groupings, authors should, as much as possible,
>
> - Make explicit their methods of categorizing human populations;
> - Define categories in as much detail as the study protocol allows;
> - Justify their choices of definitions and categories, including, for example, whether any rules of human categorization were required by their funding agency;
> - Explain whether (and if so, how) they controlled for confounding variables such as socioeconomic status, nutrition, or environmental exposures.
>
> In addition, outmoded terms and potentially stigmatizing labels should be changed

*continued*

*continued*

to more current, acceptable terminology. Examples: "Caucasian" should be changed to "white" or "of [Western] European descent" (as appropriate); "cancer victims" should be changed to "patients with cancer."

What's really interesting about these guidelines is that they're lengthy and very specific—they declare "Caucasian" outdated terminology. The editors are aware of the difference between emic and etic descriptions of self, and how people categorize their own race and ethnicity might be very different from how a researcher would identify them. But categorization goes beyond issues of race, because the editors also want to make sure that people affected by diseases aren't made into victims, as often happens with cancer, HIV, sexual assault, or domestic violence. They are instead patients with cancer, people living with HIV/AIDS (PLH), and survivors. Be careful of group labels, because participants lose their individuality (Matthews and Matthews 2008) and their humanity. "The schizophrenic" should be written as "the person diagnosed with schizophrenia." Use wording that is as neutral as possible.

For Indigenous peoples (and others), a term that is acceptable to one person on an individual basis might be offensive to someone else. While in the United States "Native Americans" is the broad term for native peoples, Canadian first inhabitants are called Aboriginal peoples. "First Nations" refers to people who are ethnically neither Métis nor Inuit (First Nations Studies Program 2009). If possible, identify the person by tribal affiliation—for example, "A Menominee woman" or, if unknown, "A Native woman." Assume that your readership is broad and diverse—this will help you think about how the wording you choose might sound to someone who is not you.

## Numbers

> Plural or singular? Writers often aren't sure about these, but here are the correct versions.
>
> | Singular | Plural |
> |----------|--------|
> | analysis | analyses |
> | anomaly | anomalies |
> | appendix | appendices |
> | criterion | criteria |
> | datum | data |
> | hypothesis | hypotheses |
> | phenomenon | phenomena |
> | stimulus | stimuli |

Whether you conduct quantitative or qualitative research, you'll need to be able to write confidently about numbers. The more precise you can be, the better.

Do not use words of size for words of significance. For example, "A big trend happening right now is . . ." Using words of size (like *big*) when you mean *importance* makes your writing look imprecise and informal.

| Incorrect | Correct |
|-----------|---------|
| Ethnic conflict is a huge problem. | Ethnic conflict is a significant problem. |

Use *between* for two things ("Between a rock and a hard place"); use *among* for three or more things, as well as to describe a population or group being studied ("HIV prevalence among men who have sex with men").

| Incorrect | Correct |
| --- | --- |
| I must choose between these alternatives: chocolate, vanilla, and strawberry. | I must choose among these alternatives: chocolate, vanilla, and strawberry. |

If things can be counted, use *few* or *many*; if they are measured but not countable, use *less* or *more*. So even though your local supermarket may have a sign that reads, "Those with less than ten items may use this line," it *should* read "Those with fewer than ten items . . ." If something can be counted, you can also say that it occurs in "greater numbers," "higher numbers," or "higher frequencies."

The words "datum" and "data" can be complicated, since "data" is actually a plural noun that today we treat as both a plural and a singular noun. I've been using it as a singular noun in this book: "how data is obtained" rather than "how data are obtained". When in doubt, treat it as a plural noun consistently throughout your paper and don't forget to match any associated words "these data," not "this data".

| Incorrect | Correct |
| --- | --- |
| There are less potsherds in this square than in that one. | There are fewer potsherds in this square than in that one. |

The digits one through ten should be written out. Higher numbers can be inserted in the text as digits—for example, "We interviewed a sample of 19 households." However, if you are beginning a sentence with a number (such as a percentage), it should be spelled out. Instead of "15 surveys arrived by

## Writing About Statistics

The excerpt below comes from the author guidelines of the medical periodical *Journal of the American Medical Association (JAMA) Internal Medicine* (JAMA Internal Medicine 2016):

> Describe statistical methods with enough detail to enable a knowledgeable reader with access to the original data to reproduce the reported results. Where sufficient data are available for both male and female subjects, separate analyses should be performed and reported for each sex.
>
> Put a general description of methods in the "Methods" section. Restrict tables and figures to those needed to explain the argument of the article and to assess its support. Avoid nontechnical uses of technical terms in statistics, such as *random* (which implies a randomizing device), *normal, significant, correlations*, and *sample*. Define statistical terms, abbreviations, and most symbols.

If you follow guidelines like these when you write about your statistics, you'll rarely encounter difficulty from an anthropological audience. The last part is especially important if your audience could include statisticians or others attuned to the specific ways that statisticians use *significant* in a technical sense (to refer to specific thresholds of probability) as opposed to the more common usages of *significant* to mean noteworthy or important.

mail," write "Fifteen surveys arrived by mail." You may also use other number words and put the more precise digits in parentheses: "Almost half (48%) of participants . . ."

Metric system units such as g, kg, km, cm, m, and so forth are not capitalized and are not followed by periods.

## Time

Anthropologists (and historians and others who work in specific time periods, for that matter) are very particular about writing about time. To an Old World archaeologist, the beginning of agriculture 12,000 years ago wasn't a very long time ago at all if you study the extinct hominin Ardipethicus, who lived about 4.4 million years ago. The Industrial Revolution, which started around 1750 AD, was a short time ago. Anthropologists have a long sense of history and timelines, and you should adopt a similar perspective. A statement that the time before computers or even smartphones was "so long ago" will ring hollow.

Depending on the subfield, paleoanthropologists and archaeologists use a variety of different time periods and dating conventions, which can get confusing. In your history class, you have probably seen time measured in years written only as BC and AD. BC means "before Christ" and AD means *Anno Domini*, "in the year of the Lord," a contraction of *Anno Domini Nostri Jesu Christi*, "in the year of our Lord Jesus Christ." Archaeological dates are often reported in the Islamic world as BH (Before the Hejira) or AH (After the Hejira), which refers to the Prophet Muhammad's departure from Mecca in September 622 CE.

Because BC and AD and BH and AH are religious time measurements, archaeologists prefer the religion-neutral dating terms BCE ("before the Common Era") and CE

## Avoid These Opening Phrases

When you are writing about time, avoid broad gener-
alities. These phrases seem especially tempting for
writers:

| | |
|---|---|
| since the beginning of time/history/ humanity | since humans walked the earth |
| from time immemorial | from the beginning |
| throughout history | for a very long time |
| since the dawn of time | for thousands of years |

Given evolution, we know that humans did not exist
at the beginning of time, so this and similar statements
are inaccurate. It is also difficult to generalize about
humans across time and space, and no one is asking you
to try. It is easier to start with a sentence that presents
your topic. If you find yourself writing a sentence with
one of the phrases above, cross it out and look more carefully at the very next sentence: It is probably much closer
to what your paper is really about.

Another clunker to avoid—as an opening phrase or
really anywhere—is "In today's society . . ."

("Common Era"). But given the competing systems, it's best
to consult your instructor about which dating conventions
to use.

BP, BC, BCE, and CE always follow the date, as in "The earliest written records we know of are from ca. 3000 BCE." AD
precedes the year, as in "AD 302."

| Other Measures/Abbreviations | Meaning |
| --- | --- |
| kyr, kybp | thousand years before present |
| kya | thousand years ago |
| myr, mybp | million years before present |
| mya | million years ago |
| BCE | before the Common Era |
| CE | Common Era |
| BP | before present (1950) |

You might also need to pay attention to whether or not the abbreviations are in upper or lower case, because lower case means the date was derived by radiocarbon methods and reflects radiocarbon years rather than calendar years.

## Gendered Language

Anthropologists have had a longstanding commitment to awareness of more than two genders and the complexities of how the human experience is gendered. As gender is a shifting terrain, it is not always easy to know what to do with pronouns or other words out of a desire to not offend anyone. Gendered language is language that favors one gender over another. As anthropologists we have a responsibility to counteract inequality in language by thinking carefully about the pronouns we use, especially the use of androcentric words such as "mankind" or taking phrases such as "all men are created equal" at face value. Archaeologist K. Anne Pyburn (2008) writes about the efforts of archaeologists to revolutionize the framework about how women are discussed in the archaeological record instead of trying to "add women and stir."

The Society for American Archaeology's Journal Style Guide (Society for American Archaeology 2014) states that the society adheres to the 1973 AAA statement on gender-inclusive language, which "discourages the employment of male third-person pronouns and the use of generic 'man' in reference to non-sex-specific semantic categories. More comprehensive terms (e.g., 'one,' 'person,' 'humans,' 'humankind,' 'they'), in grammatically correct constructions, are preferred as a matter of equity." Sweden added a gender-neutral pronoun, "hen," to its dictionary to refer to the gender of someone who is transgender or transitioning, or someone whose gender is unknown (Villarreal 2015). But English is not so lucky. "S/he," "she/he," and "he/she" tend to annoy readers, so the most common convention is to make both the pronoun and the antecedent plural. In English grammar there is a recognition that there are more than two genders; "they" is increasingly acceptable as a singular gender-non-specific pronoun.

For example, instead of

> Every good writer should know how he can convert pronouns to the plural. [correct in singular–plural consistency but *not* gender-inclusive]

or

> Every good writer should know how he or she can convert pronouns to the plural. [correct in singular–plural consistency but indicates the two-gender dichotomy and is also clunky when read aloud]

try

> All writers should know how they can convert pronouns to the plural. [correct in singular–plural consistency, gender-inclusive, and much less clunky]

These are simple revisions that are actually easier for the writer and promote gender equality.

Here is a list of commonly used nouns and their gender-neutral alternatives.

| Gendered Noun | Gender-Neutral Noun |
| --- | --- |
| man | person, individual |
| freshman | first-year student |
| co-ed | student |
| mankind | people, humans, human beings, humanity |
| manmade | machine-made, synthetic |
| the common man | the average (or ordinary) person |
| to man | to operate, to cover, to staff |
| chairman | chair, chairperson, coordinator |
| mailman | mail carrier, letter carrier, postal worker |
| policeman | police officer |
| steward, stewardess | flight attendant |
| congressman | congress person, legislator, representative |
| Dear Sir: | To Whom it May Concern: Dear Editor:, Dear Service Representative:, Dear Committee Members: |

I have seen students refer to male authors by their last names but female authors by their first names. Refer to all researchers by their last names and titles, regardless of their gender.

## Use of "I"

One "rule" that students in the United States often carry with them from high school to college is "Never use *I* in academic writing." This maxim is simple and memorable—it is often rooted in a fear that using "I" will open the floodgates to personal gushing—but the rule simply doesn't hold up in academic life. Scholars who publish in a variety of academic fields, including anthropology, regularly use "I" or "we." For example, the author guidelines for *Nature*, one of the top science journals, suggest that authors write, "Here we show" to start a concluding paragraph in a research article.

In the introductions to social science articles, you'll regularly see "I argue," "I present," "I begin," "I use." When composing reading responses, students frequently use "I think" and "I believe" at the beginning of the sentences. These are fine ways to start a sentence—they are ways of claiming your ideas and maintaining active voice—but *overusing* such "metadiscourse" can erode your credibility, make you appear to be pleading too much. This is particularly relevant for women (Carli 1990), who tend to use more metadiscourse than men in their communication, and frequent use of "I think" and "I believe" could be interpreted as overly deferential. Pronouns are small but powerful words, and they need to be deployed precisely.

Here is an example of a writer who avoids using "I," awkwardly:

> While reading the article, "Unpacking the Invisible Knapsack II: Sexual Orientation", the authors cited many daily effects of straight privilege that unfortunately seemed quite true. Many statements that were made by the heterosexually-identified Earlham College students were aspects of daily life that "straight" people take for granted. After reading the article some statements seemed extremely bothersome to me.

The writer in this example avoids "I" awkwardly in several sentences. The first sentence involves a "dangling participle" because the subject should be "I," the student who is doing the reading, not the authors. An alternative could be, "While reading the Invisible Knapsack, I noticed that the authors cited . . ." The final sentence could be recast as "I was bothered by . . ."

Both of the following examples use "I" to make strong statements. The second sentence is better, however, because it uses "I" sparingly. Although it is a longer sentence, it includes more specifics about writer's argument.

> **Good**: In this paper I will analyze Fernea's fieldwork methods as well as the role of religion in Islamic society. I believe that Fernea gave a very accurate and detailed portrayal of life in El Nahra, and I will show how religion plays a very important role in social organization and control especially towards women.

> **Better**: She acquired a unique perspective of the role of females in a patrilineal Shiite tribal society and thus, I believe Elizabeth Warnock Fernea's ethnography, *Guests of the Sheik*, provides substantial evidence that the laws of Purdah create a functional and many times beneficial lifestyle for the women of El Nahra, and establishes them as the foundation for the sustenance, stability, and continuation of society.

## Being Concise

Concision is about choosing the most powerful words and writing lean, efficient sentences. The following sentence is grammatically correct but bloated with unnecessary words. A good first move is to simply cross out all the filler and repetition:

Among the many ways that one can illustrate and show cutting wordiness and improving concision is by simply using the crossout tool of this word processing program to show

how many ~~needless and~~ unnecessary words can be cut by a careful editor ~~who scrutinizes the text~~.

But don't stop there. Also consider whether rearranging parts of the sentence could make the passage more concise:

To illustrate just how many unnecessary words a careful editor can cut, one can use the crossout tool.

Some further strategies for concision:

- Read your prose aloud and note where you run out of breath, pause, or stumble. Revisit those spots and try to say what you want to say more plainly.
- Delete meaningless words (e.g., actually, kind of, really, quite) and doubled words (e.g., true and accurate, first and foremost, basic and fundamental).
- Delete what readers can infer (e.g., ~~future~~ plans, ~~true~~ facts, ~~free~~ gift, ~~each~~ individual, ~~final~~ outcome, red ~~in color~~, large ~~in size~~, ~~the field~~ of anthropology).
- Replace common (but pretentious) phrases with better (and shorter) alternatives:

| Replace . . . | With . . . |
|---|---|
| Due to the fact that | Because |
| In the event that | If |
| At the time of | When |
| People working in the field of anthropology | Anthropologists |
| At those times when you are going out to the field to do fieldwork | When doing fieldwork |

Here's an example of a wordy sentence written by a student:

It may be a natural tendency for the Western mind to analyze the position of women in an Iraqi Shiite tribal culture and view the veiling and seclusion as repression rather than protection from strangers and their thoughts; or the act of consummating a marriage, in which the women look at the sheets for blood to determine whether the bride was a virgin, as invasive, rather than necessary to ensure the purity of a family's lineage. Such is the nature of ethnocentrism.

← The subject and verb are far apart: "difficulty . . . is."

← The semicolon use doubles the sentence length, but the semicolon is not the real problem.

← "Western mind" is broad and imprecise since we do not know what "Western" means.

← There is a problem of parallelism since what comes after "or" doesn't grammatically match what comes before it.

How about this as an improvement?

> When Iraqi Shiite women wear veils, seclude themselves, and inspect bed sheets to confirm a bride's virginity, some Westerners get insulted, but that seems to me ethnocentric.

In this case (as in many cases), converting the sentence from passive voice to active voice made it more concise.

## Active and Passive Voice

You may have heard the rule, "Do not use passive voice." In passive voice, the subject is *receiving* the action, and it becomes less clear who or what is doing the action. Sentences that include "to be" verbs—*is, are, was, were, be*—are usually passive.

**Passive**: A grant proposal to the National Science Foundation was written by us.

**Active**: We wrote a National Science Foundation grant proposal.
**Passive**: Semi-structured interviews were conducted with participants.
**Active**: I conducted semi-structured interviews with participants.
**Passive**: It is believed by the Warlpiri people of Australia that each Ancestral Being is connected to a geographic territory.
**Active**: The Warlpiri people of Australia believe that each Ancestral Being inhabits a geographic territory.

Some students think that passive sentences sound smarter or project a more objective voice, but that's just not the case. When in doubt, use active voice—readers generally find such sentences easier to comprehend. English sentence structure is typically subject—verb—object, so brains oriented to the English language think in terms of a *subject/character doing something* and intuitively expect a subject—verb—object sentence construction.

Tedlock and Kepp (2005) offer this advice: "Search your draft for every sentence written in the passive voice ('The wonderful story was written by you') and ask yourself whether it needs to be that way for a good reason, such as creating variety of sentence structure in a paragraph. If not, rewrite it in active voice ('You wrote the story that touched my heart')." They also note the ethical reason for preferring the active voice: "This not only makes more interesting reading but also forces you to identify the 'agent' of the action in the sentence" (36).

Do not be afraid to use "I" or "we" to take ownership of what you are writing about. Social scientists, and certainly anthropologists, value displaying their agency as researchers and showing the relationship between concepts or variables clearly. In this sense, active voice can contribute not only to reader comprehension (and, as noted earlier, to concision) but also to reflexivity.

## Verbs

Perhaps even more important than preferring the active voice is seeking out the most *precise* verbs in any given sentence. Scientists tend to recycle the same words and phrases. Matthews and Matthews (2008) note that "scientists often write as though only seven verbs exist" (139): demonstrate, exhibit, present, observe, occur, report, and show.

Incorporate more than just these into your writing, but before you get too creative, learn to use these words appropriately. Keep in mind that for these verbs, authors should perform the action, not the studies or papers themselves: not "The research found" but instead "The authors found" (Smyth 2004). It seems natural to want to anthropomorphize texts, but do not ascribe action to inanimate resources.

Notice how the verbs in the revised sentence below are more active, more precise, and more purposeful:

| Original | Revised |
|---|---|
| This section is the literature review and the next one is about Foucault's theory. | After reviewing the relevant literature, I challenge Foucault's argument by ... |

The lists below give you a running start on widening your repertoire of verbs. If you learn to recognize the differences among these (and the many more available to you), you'll not only be able to understand more quickly what any assignment is asking you to do but also deploy more precise and purposeful verbs in your own prose.

## Information Words

Information words ask you to demonstrate what you know about the subject, such as who, what, when, where, how, and why (Writing Center 2012).

**define**—give the subject's meaning (according to someone or something). Sometimes you have to give more than one view on the subject's meaning.

**explain**—give reasons why or examples of how something happened

**illustrate**—give descriptive examples of the subject and show how each is connected with the subject

**list**—order facts, attributes, or items in sequence

**outline**—organize according to hierarchy and/or category

**research**—gather material from outside sources about the subject, often with the implication or requirement that you will analyze what you have found

**review**—reexamine the main points or highlights of something

**state**—assert with confidence

**summarize**—briefly list the important ideas you learned about the subject

**trace**—outline how something has changed or developed from an earlier time to its current form

## Relation Words

Relation words ask you to demonstrate how things are connected.

**apply**—use details that you have been given to demonstrate how an idea, theory, or concept works in a particular situation

**cause**—show how one event or series of events made something else happen

**compare**—show how two or more things are similar (and, sometimes, different)
**contrast**—show how two or more things are dissimilar
**relate**—show or describe the connections between things

## Interpretation Words

Interpretation words ask you to defend ideas of your own about the subject. Do not see these words as requesting opinion alone (unless the assignment specifically says so), but as requiring opinion that is supported by concrete evidence. Remember examples, principles, definitions, or concepts from class or research and use them in your interpretation.

**analyze**—determine how individual parts create or relate to the whole; figure out how something works, what it might mean, or why it is important
**argue, challenge**—take a side and defend it with evidence against the other side
**assess**—summarize your opinion of the subject and measure it against something
**critique**—point out both positive and negative aspects
**describe**—show what something looks like, including physical features
**discuss**—explore an issue from all sides; implies wide latitude
**evaluate, respond**—state your opinion of the subject as good, bad, or some combination of the two, with examples and reasons
**interpret**—translate how or why; implies some subjective judgment
**justify**—give reasons or examples to demonstrate how or why something is the truth
**support**—give reasons or evidence for something you believe (be sure to state clearly what it is that you believe)

**synthesize**—put two or more things together that have not been put together in class or in your readings before. Do not just summarize one and then the other and say that they are similar or different; provide a reason for putting them together that runs all the way through the paper.

## Verb Tenses

The tense of verbs is a subtle but important convention for showing the status of the work being reported (Matthews and Matthews 2008, 48–50). The table below shows which tenses are appropriate for the section of a proposal or report (however, the exact conventions may vary by academic journal).

|              | Proposal                                        | IMRD Report        |
| ------------ | ----------------------------------------------- | ------------------ |
| Abstract     | Present OR past, depending on type of abstract  | Present or past    |
| Introduction | Present and past                                | Present and past   |
| Methods      | Future                                          | Past               |
| Results      | N/A                                             | Past               |
| Discussion   | N/A                                             | Present and past   |
| Conclusion   | Future                                          | Present, future    |

Use present tense when a fact has been published, because facts are established knowledge, and cite the source: *Anthropologists study language in its social context.*

Use present tense when describing a theorist's ideas, even if the theorist is dead and the work was written in the past: *Karl Marx insists that class struggles are connected to labor.*

Use present perfect tense for repeated events, for actions beginning in the past and continuing into the present: *Anthropologists have studied language in this way for only the past two decades.*

Use past tense to describe actual historical events: *Karl Marx published "The Communist Manifesto" in 1848.*

Use past tense to discuss results that cannot be generalized. When a finding in a source is very specific, use past tense because this is work from a study that was already conducted: *The hypothesis was confirmed by this research.*

Use the past tense for unpublished results (e.g., preliminary findings): *Preliminary findings identified discrepancies between the two tests.*

Use the present tense to refer readers to your figures and tables: *Table 3 presents demographic information on the participants.*

Use past tense in the discussion section to summarize the findings or the study itself, but use present tense for generalizing, describing implications of the research, and making conclusions: *The purpose of this study was to explore individuals' attitudes toward religion. . . . Attitudes toward religion seem to be related to first childhood experiences attending religious services.*

## Transitions

Any writer can fall into a rut by using the same transitions over and over; better writers draw on a wide repertoire of transitional words and phrases. They use them to introduce variety, but, more importantly, they select the most precise transition for the given purpose. Here are some of your options.

To *extend or add to an idea*:

| | | | |
|---|---|---|---|
| again | even more | furthermore | moreover |
| also | finally | in addition | next |
| and, or, nor | first | in the first, second place | second, secondly |
| besides | further | last, lastly | too |

To *draw contrast*:

| | | | |
|---|---|---|---|
| at the same time | in contrast | notwithstanding | otherwise |
| but | nevertheless | on the contrary | though |
| however | nonetheless | on the other hand | yet |

To *clarify*:

in other words
i.e., (that is)
to clarify

To *signal cause and effect*:

| Cause | Effect |
|---|---|
| because | accordingly |
| for that reason | as a result |
| on account of | consequently |
| since | hence |
| | therefore, thus |

To *conclude*:

finally
in conclusion
in short
in summary
to conclude

## Improving Flow

Employing precise transitions is one important way to improve flow, but not the only way. Your reader's ability to understand what you are communicating depends on how readily he or she can connect words within sentences, sentences within paragraphs, and paragraphs to other paragraphs. You can improve the flow in three more ways.

First, *use some key words from the assignment* in your introductory paragraph. By echoing some of the same phrases (only *a few*, not all!), you are echoing the original assignment in a way that will appeal to your readers by putting them on familiar ground. Let's say your assignment is a movie critique:

In this paper you will be applying anthropology to popular culture. This assignment is intended for you to use course concepts to visualize, **identify**, and **critique** popular media. You can discuss what the movie **portrays** as well as how the movie portrays it, meaning you can discuss the **culture**(s) portrayed in the movie and/ or discuss the culture of moviemaking as illustrated in the movie.

You could start your paper this way:

Director James Cameron is famous for his **popular** and flashy blockbuster films such as *The Terminator*, *Titanic*, and *Avatar*, which have grossed over a billion dollars combined. These films, however, are usually heavier on special effects and weaker on plot. *Avatar* in particular is the visually

← Notice the use of key verbs and nouns from the assignment prompt.

← Notice the use of compliment and critique of the film and filmmaker.

stunning film in which a paralyzed soldier is transported to an alien world threatened by humans searching for metals. Although he first experiences *culture shock*, he becomes a *participant-observer* among the Na'vi people. He eventually not only becomes committed to their cause but also becomes their lead warrior in the fight against the humans. Apart from the environmental messaging, the film uses aliens and their plight to appeal to viewers' humanity by **portraying** an invented anthropomorphic species that actually most closely resembles North American Native Americans. This paper **identifies and critiques** the way the aliens are purposefully designed to resemble humans but reinforces stereotypes of the "other" and the "noble savage" through the **portrayal** of Na'vi **culture**.

Second, *progress from old to new information.* Joseph M. Williams (1990) has been a pioneer in helping us understand that readers need to graft new information onto what they already know—and that this dynamic is at work even at the sentence level. That means that writers should construct sentences that move from "what is familiar or simple" to "what is new or complex"—or what he calls from "old" to "new" information. Here's a simple example:

| Original | Revised |
|---|---|
| Cultural anthropology, biological anthropology, linguistic anthropology and archaeology are the four major subfields. | The four major subfields are cultural anthropology, biological anthropology, linguistic anthropology, and archaeology. |

Both sentences are grammatically correct, but the writer of the original is making things harder on readers than necessary because we must quickly reprocess the front end of the sentence in light of what we learn at the end. Better to put the simpler/older/more familiar information ("the four major subfields are . . .") *first* so that it can frame what comes later.

| Original | Revised |
|---|---|
| Moving simpler or more familiar information to the front of a sentence and more complex or "newer" material to the end of a sentence is something that can be done by writers to improve the readability of their sentences. Not starting sentences with long, abstract subjects is recommended by Williams as a way to improve flow, also. That humans learn by grafting new information to their existing knowledge schemas, which is a long-established principle of cognitive science, helps to explain why both of those style strategies for cohesion improve readability. | To improve readability, writers can move simple or familiar information to the front of a sentence and complex or newer information to the end. Also, Williams warns against starting sentences with long, abstract subjects. Both of these style strategies improve flow because people learn by grafting new information to existing knowledge schemas. This is a long-established principle of cognitive science. |

Always ask, *Can I rearrange the sentence to make it match the way readers will actually process the information?* In this case, the revised version follows the old-to-new principle. Notice as well that the writer converted most of the sentences to active voice, employed more precise verbs, and applied the tips for concision—all of which were covered earlier in this chapter.

Finally, *link sentences with similar words*. To improve flow, start a fair percentage of sentences with words that echo those you used to conclude the previous sentence. This trick is helpful for building a logical argument and connecting the ideas within a paragraph. Here's an example:

> The **Immigration Act** of 1924 reinforced American nativist ideas by limiting the total number of immigrants to the United States through a permanent quota **system**. This **system** built upon previous **immigration acts** by reinforcing eugenic ideas that stated that some **ethnic groups** were better workers and less prone to undesirable hereditary traits than other **ethnic immigrant groups**. Potential **immigrants** from Asia were restricted from coming to the United States, and the quota system did not apply to other countries in the Western Hemisphere such as **Mexico** and Canada. **Mexico**, for example, provided inexpensive labor to the United States during World War I.

Notice how the bolded words create links. Now, you wouldn't want to continue this lockstep pattern throughout an essay—that could become tiresome for readers—but this strategy can be helpful as for editing those patches of text that strike you as choppy or disconnected, especially when you are stuck on how to make the flow more logical and smooth.

## Parallelism

Parallelism is about symmetry and balance—it speaks to our hankering for logic and order. All of the sentences below are grammatically adequate, but those on the left that violate parallelism are stylistically lazy.

| Not Parallel | Parallel |
|---|---|
| <u>To maintain</u> parallelism in constructions is like <u>fulfilling</u> a contract with readers: They expect **consistency** and **sentences that are logically constructed**. | <u>Maintaining</u> parallelism is like <u>fulfilling</u> a contract with readers: They expect **consistently designed** and **logically constructed** sentences. <br><br> <u>To maintain</u> parallelism is <u>to fulfill</u> a contract with readers: They expect sentence structures that are **consistent** and **logical**. |

All three of those sentences are grammatically correct, but only the two on the right reveal an understanding of parallel structure. Notice that there is usually more than one way to make a sentence more parallel.

Here are three common writing situations that call for particular attention to parallelism:

### "Not Only . . . But Also"

Make sure you follow "not only" with "but also" (not just "but"). Moreover, make elements following each of those conjunctions as parallel in syntax as possible (perfect parallelism is not always possible). The same principles apply to "either/or" and "neither/nor" constructions.

| Flawed Parallelism | Improved Parallelism |
|---|---|
| Not only <u>did the author learn about the men's feelings towards overconfidence and arrogance</u>, but <u>it was learned first-hand how an overconfident person is eventually deflated</u>. | The author learned not only <u>about the men's feelings toward overconfidence and arrogance</u> but also <u>about how an overconfident person is likely to be eventually deflated</u>. |

The author learned not only about <u>how men feel about overconfidence and arrogance</u> but also <u>how they end up deflated when they persistently express overconfidence</u>. The author not only <u>surveyed how men felt about overconfidence and arrogance</u> but also <u>explained how those who persistently express overconfidence end up deflated</u>.

## Repetitive Clauses

The example that opens this section is keyed to repetitive clauses, but here's another example:

| Flawed Parallelism | Improved Parallelism |
|---|---|
| Until recently, researchers mistakenly believed that <u>hunting was performed predominantly by men</u> and <u>gatherers were only women.</u> | Until recently, researchers mistakenly believed that <u>men engaged mainly in hunting</u> and <u>women mainly in gathering</u>. |
| | Until recently, researchers mistakenly believed that <u>men hunted</u> and <u>women gathered.</u> |

## Items in a Series

This should be an easy one, but too many careless writers overlook it, much to the annoyance of careful readers. Note that the principle applies equally to sentences and bullets.

| Flawed Parallelism | Improved Parallelism |
|---|---|
| Sedentary humans can become more active by <u>walking as much as possible</u>, <u>take up biking around the neighborhood</u>, and <u>run for aerobic exercise</u>. | Sedentary humans can be more active by <u>walking as much as possible</u>, <u>biking around the neighborhood</u>, and <u>running for aerobic exercise</u>. |
| There are several ways you can improve your style: <br>• Active voice <br>• Make sentences more concise <br>• Improving transitions <br>• Parallelism | There are several ways to improve your style: <br>• Employ the active voice <br>• Make sentences more concise <br>• Improve transitions <br>• Check parallelism |

Parallelism matches form to meaning and creates logical consistency—it can also generate aesthetically pleasing rhythm and balance.

## Sentence and Paragraph Length

Any anthropologist can probably name five scholars whose sentences are so long and jargon-filled that the text is nearly impossible to get through. Their names will remain anonymous to protect the guilty.

Sentence length is important for comprehension: too long and you lose your reader, too short and you look juvenile or condescending. Most readers do not see a string of long, complicated phrases as impressive; instead, they find it taxing. If you stick entirely to short sentences, however, readers are likely to get irked by the staccato rhythm or to think your prose is too simplistic. Matthews and Matthews (2008) suggest that sentences should be 15 to 20 words long for optimal readability.

Sentence variety, however, is also important because varying the sentence length and kind keeps readers interested and motivated to read more. Consider the following two paragraphs by Arthur Kleinman, Professor of Medical Anthropology and Cross Cultural Psychiatry at Harvard University:

My odyssey of academic and popular publication has been a search for a voice: a style of representing my ideas and projects that seemed original, enabling, comfortable, and authentic. That demanding and at times perplexing quest has taken me down dead ends, along streets that circle back on their origin, across unchartered intersections, through confusing neighborhoods where frankly I got lost, and also in more promising directions. In 1973 at the end of several years of post-doctoral fellowship at Harvard, I published four articles which largely framed my career interests for the next quarter century. Those articles varied significantly in writing style because I found myself constrained by both theory and findings: pulled then in the direction of greater technical detail; pushed occasionally to present models in a more generalizable theoretical language; but not once finding the right balance or cadence or beauty. Indeed, I then distrusted prose that seemed either stylized or overly attractive.

Over the years, my style has gotten more spare. I use fewer adjectives. I emphasize active verbs. I am more comfortable with fewer nouns, and with ones that are the most concrete. I prune sentences more severely, and have learned to be less tolerant of long ones with compound thoughts and phrases. I feel less pressure to be comprehensive or complete, and more to be simple and direct, and to write in a coherent and compelling way. I always have written out by hand multiple drafts; maybe not the 15 or 16 that the late Susan Sontag somewhere claimed she wrote; yet more than one or two. The physical act of writing is pleasing, but also the only way I can think through things in depth. My first book, *Patients and Healers in the Context of Culture*, was 427 pages; my last, *What Really Matters*, is 260 pages. My published articles are also more concise. At 67 years of age, perhaps I have less to say that seems original and useful; or maybe I have found a voice that is more disciplined, more contained.

(You can find this and similar reflections by distinguished scholars at "Writers on Writing" page of Durham University's Writing Across Boundaries project: https://www.dur.ac.uk/writingacrossboundaries/ writingonwriting/.)

Kleinman's longest sentence is 56 words, his shortest 4. That is no accident. Notice how the sentence in which he declares that his style has gotten spare is, well, spare, and how the sentence that recounts his feeling lost is long but includes several short clauses, inviting readers into the circling, halting, wandering feeling of getting lost. He employs repetition and parallelism strategically. Notice as well the variety in punctuation—he uses colons and semicolons (you might also consider dashes and parentheses).

Even a paragraph that includes this kind of dazzling variety in sentence structure should focus on a single idea. Matthews and Matthews (2008) suggest that 150 words is optimal for most paragraphs in published scientific articles (Kleinman's paragraphs above are 155 and 184). You can easily check word counts using the tool in your word processor, but just as valuable is your eye: If one paragraph occupies an entire page, break it into smaller paragraphs. Likewise, if you have a string of two- or three-sentence paragraphs, they are probably too thin.

## Jargon

In an effort to control jargon, some style guidelines shrilly warn, "Avoid jargon!" or "Use jargon-free, simple language." As the Calvin and Hobbes cartoon suggests, often such prohibitions are often well founded. Never drop the terms into your

FIGURE 6.1 Because None of Us Have *Ever* Tried to Impress Someone with our Words, Right?

sentences to impress. And do not assume that technical terms can stand in for good argument or analysis.

Yet technical terms help us do the work of our discipline— they are frequently *part* of good argument and analysis—and you would be wise to incorporate in your own prose some specialized terminology, especially terms discussed in lectures and found in your course books.

One fairly reliable strategy for weaving (good) jargon into your own writing is to employ appositive phrases—that is, you define the term in a clause or phrase (or occasionally a whole sentence) immediately after you introduce it. This serves three purposes: (1) It considers the needs of your readers, especially if you think some of them may not be familiar with the term; (2) it helps you test whether *you* really understand the term; and (3) it proves to your instructor that you understand the term (this last reason applies *only* to school/student writing). Notice the placement of appositives in these three passages:

> The artifact was photographed *in situ* —that is, in its original place on the site.
> Archaeologists incorporate principles of geology such as stratigraphy, the layering of deposits in archaeological sites. The benefits of understanding stratigraphy include . . .
> The Shiites in the El Nahra are endogamists since they prefer to marry within their tribe. The mothers of the men select their son's first wife and he can then choose to take on another wife if he pleases.

After initially defining a specialized term with an appositive, you can use the term on its own throughout the rest of the paper.

# Commonly Misused Words

## Obvious, Normal/Norm, Traditional

Remember cultural relativism and reflexivity, introduced in Chapter 1? Your writing style should be informed by anthropological values. All three of these misused words relate to how the writer relates to the reader. Don't assume that the reader is just like you, sharing the same or even similar cultural, ethnic, racial, class, and gender backgrounds. Don't assume that the reader will understand what is normal for you. Instead, take the time to explain the idea. "Normal" and "traditional" need context to make practical or ethical sense.

| Flawed | Better |
|---|---|
| On this holiday, people eat traditional foods. | On this holiday, people eat traditional Greek foods such as tzatziki and feta. |
| Participants engaged in normal activities. | Participants engaged in normal Saturday afternoon activities like housework, cooking, and going to the movies. |
| The author made his argument obvious. | The author made his argument obvious very early in the paper, in the second paragraph. |

## Primitive

Labeling people as *primitive* used to be a hallmark of anthropology, a shorthand for organizing peoples and cultures. The subtitle to Margaret Mead's 1928 *Coming of Age in Samoa* reads, "A Psychological Study of Primitive Youth for Western Civilization." Anthropology has historically studied non-industrial peoples, and the word "primitive" conjures stereotypical and offensive images of loincloths, stone tools, and a bone in the nose. By the 1950s, anthropologists were rethinking terminology such as "primitive" and "native." Now fast-forward to 2007 when the Association of Social Anthropologists issued a statement that definitively condemned "primitive" and "Stone Age":

> All anthropologists would agree that the negative use of the terms 'primitive' and 'Stone Age' to describe [tribal peoples] has serious implications for their welfare. Governments and other social groups . . . have long used these ideas as a pretext for depriving such peoples of land and other resources. (Khazaleh 2007)

It's best to simply avoid "primitive."

## Fuzzy Nouns

Once a student asked me, "How do you describe a thing?" At first, it seemed like an odd question: She knew that "thing" is not exactly what she meant, but she wasn't sure of how to describe something. "Thing" is just too vague and juvenile when there are better alternatives. Choose one or two of the following words, use it in the introduction, and keep using it throughout the paper. Don't try to use too many of these words, though. Because they are abstract, your reader will think you're introducing a new concept each time you use a new kind of word from this family. But remember, these words are not exactly interchangeable. In the introduction, try to be as precise as you can, even though you are just introducing main ideas. Being too broad in an introduction can backfire: "Since the beginning of time/Since the dawn of humankind" sentences will never work in an anthro course. You're not writing a movie trailer—you're writing an introduction!

| concept | idea | meaning |
| construct | issue | phenomenon |

Anthropologists love the word "phenomenon." "Issue" is also good for trying to identify the intricacies in a human problem. However, don't use it to mean "problem" as in "He has issues"—think "dilemma" instead. Also, "findings" is not exactly the same as results. "Findings" refers to the broader "what did you find as a result of doing the research?" "Results" should refer to the outcome of the study.

Matthews and Matthews (2008) consider the following nouns "fuzzy" because they aren't usually strong enough to carry the sentence on their own:

| area | character | | conditions | field |
| issue | level | nature | problem | |
| process | situation | structure | system | |

These words usually need additional modifiers to qualify, define, and restrict their breadth.

## Commonly Misused Homophones
When academic readers see these words misused, they usually wince.

accept (verb meaning to consent to receive or believe as valid)

I will not accept the idea that *Homo floresiensis* is extinct.

except (a preposition or conjunction meaning not including)

I like all vegetables, except for asparagus.

rite (noun meaning ceremony or act)

Upon completion of the rite of passage, the
adolescents became adults in that culture.
right (as a noun, a moral or legal entitlement)
According to the United Nations, education is a
human right.
who's (a contraction for "who is")
Who's going to survive the next global epidemic?
whose (a possessive)
Do you know whose book was left behind in class?
you're (a contraction for "you are")
You're going to study several subcultures.
your (a possessive)
Your values are shaped by your culture.
it's (a contraction for "it is")
It's important to use gender-inclusive pronouns.
its (a possessive)
Do not judge a book by its cover.

## The Thesaurus as Your Frenemy

The thesaurus is both your friend and your enemy: It can help or hurt you. If you find yourself repeating the same word and can't think of alternatives, certainly consult a thesaurus—it helps generate more variety in your word choice. Then again, you might be tempted to replace simple words with more complex, seemingly impressive ones: *prodigious* for *large*, *numerous* for *many*, *enfeebled* for *ill*, *lugubrious* for *sad*. Resist the urge— the simpler choice is usually the better one.

Sometimes the thesaurus will lead you to a more precise word than the one you were using, and that is terrific. But this can work in the opposite direction too. For example, "plethora" means "oversupply," but is mostly used to mean "a lot." If you write of a "plethora of partygoers" in your paper, you will come across not as smart but instead as amateurish.

## Relationships Between Elements

The first thing to know about comparisons is that it is never enough to state that a pair of words or concepts are simply "related" or "interrelated." Everything's related in anthropology—that's the holistic part. Here are some questions to ask yourself about what the relationship is between the two concepts or items that you are comparing:

How much of each is there?

Is the amount adequate? Or is there . . .

← These "not enough" words are important for research proposals and literature reviews where you are pointing out gaps.

| Too Much | Not Enough |
|---|---|
| excess | paucity |
| glut | scarcity |
| ample | dearth |
| surplus | deficiency |

Are the two things correlated? As one thing increases or decreases, do you notice an increase or decrease in the other? If you notice an increase or decrease, can you further describe it?

Remember that comparative and superlative adjectives require evidence. When you use an adjective, it suggests to the reader that this is either your opinion or a fact. Either way, you need to provide context and/or link this to evidence for the

## Beware of Exaggeration

The following words are commonly used for emphasis in student papers. Use them judiciously. If you overuse them, readers may perceive you as exaggerating.

crucial
especially
significantly
urgently
prove/proven
definitely
absolutely

statement. For example, "the Empire State Building was the tallest building in the world." Write instead, "Built in the 1930s, the Empire State Building was the tallest building in the world for 41 years" (www.esbnyc.com). We will discuss in the next chapter the full range of how to cite sources.

# CITING YOUR SOURCES

7

When you cite, you show that you are building on the research of others. You are also differentiating your voice from the voices of others. Can documenting sources with in-text citations and references lists be tedious? Sure. But not attending to documentation conventions suggests to readers both a deficit of disciplinary knowledge and a lack of care.

Citations and references are partly about showing that you have paid attention to detail and partly about signaling your emerging membership in a disciplinary community. Depending on the subfield, timespan, and region they study, archaeologists use formats governed by the American Anthropological Association (AAA), the Society for American Archaeology (SAA), or one of several journals: *American Antiquity* (AmAntiq), *American Journal of Physical Anthropology* (AJPA), *Journal of Animal Science* (JAS), and *Journal of Human Evolution* (JHE). Each has its own style and rules about capitalization, numbering, punctuation, tables, and creating your list of references.

The most common style is AAA, and as of September 2015, AAA style adheres fully to *The Chicago Manual of Style* (author-date version). You might think, "Can't I just use the style I'm more familiar with, like the MLA style I learned in English classes? I mean, if I'm giving the author credit, that's what's most important, right?" Yes, giving authors credit *is* the

## What Counts as Common Knowledge?

Students are often confused about when they do not need to cite an idea that's in the public domain (i.e., widely accepted as fact). The phrase "nature versus nurture" is in the public domain, even though the answer to this debate is still not known. In archaeology, stratigraphy, the idea that fossils found deeper in the dirt are older than fossils closer to the surface, is considered fact. You can also hedge your statement with phrases such as "generally accepted as," "generally accepted that, " or "it is widely known that" (Smyth 2004). If you are ever in doubt, cite the source. Students risk plagiarism when they paraphrase without acknowledging the original author. It is easier to show a track record of your research than have to prove it later.

most important part, but learning the citation conventions of a particular discipline—and following them—is a must if you wish to move deeper into that community.

## Fabrication and Plagiarism

Fabrication involves making up data. Plagiarism involves using another author's language and thoughts without properly giving credit. Both constitute serious academic misconduct. Sometimes plagiarism is accidental; sometimes it is intentional. In either case, you are accountable.

To stay on the right side of academic integrity, you should:

- Recognize what is common knowledge, because it does not need to be cited.
- Err on the side of caution and include citations when you are not sure if something is common knowledge.

- Select direct quotations strategically and introduce them with lead-in or signal phrases.
- Know that you need to cite a source even if you summarize or paraphrase it rather than directly quote it.
- Become a good paraphraser who can compress the original text and express it in your own words and syntax (trading out a few words of a quotation and inserting some replacements of your own is *not* a permissible paraphrase, even if you provide a citation).

This chapter will assist you in all five of those activities. Your institution or instructor may have additional policies, such as a code of conduct or guidelines for using plagiarism-checking software.

## Consider Adding an Acknowledgment Section

It is very important to acknowledge everyone who helped you on your research product. Anthropologists nowadays work in teams, collaborating with other professionals with different research backgrounds, or senior professors with their graduate student advisees. The picture of the lone anthropologist working in the field is a romanticized idea. Colin Turnbull's 1961 ethnography *The Forest People* (1961) downplayed the researchers who came to live with the Pygmies before he did and who helped him identify a group to live with. According to his biographer Roy Richard Grinker (2000), Turnbull exaggerated the amount of time he spent in the field and omitted mentions of the help he received, in order to fit

*continued*

continued
the style of cultural anthropologists' ethnographic writing. Grinker writes:

> Although many anthropologists would likely
> disapprove of Colin's attempts to overstate his
> solitude and fieldwork time, few would be
> surprised. Cultural anthropologists, especially
> those who are unmarried, have long been
> expected to work alone, without teams of re-
> searchers and usually without much contact
> with other 'outsiders.' For the purposes of
> Colin's credibility, the less Colin said about
> Newton, the better. Anthropologists habitually
> exaggerate: the longer the time in the field, the
> more authenticity the anthropologist believes he
> or she gains. Those who shared in Colin's experi-
> ences thus went unrecognized (2000, 108–109).

Luckily, today, there's less pressure in the anthropology community to make it look like you did your work all alone, and team research continues to grow in popularity.

Thank your participants (even if you can't name them, out of maintaining confidentiality). Many publications and nearly all theses include a statement that acknowledges those who contributed to the project. Even as an undergraduate, you can and should acknowledge people who participated in your research. Because of confidentiality, you will not name them individually, but you should include a broad sentence to cover them. For example:

> "We would like to thank the individuals who
> generously donated their time for this
> research."

> "We are extremely grateful to the research
> participants for lending their time and
> experience to this project."
> "We thank the individuals who participated in
> this research."
>
> This can be done in a preface, a footnote, or before the
> references.

A more mundane, less high-profile data problem is the act of simply seeing more in your data than is actually there. Since the cultural anthropologist is the instrument of data collection in participant observation, the risk of seeing something that is not there may be higher than in other disciplines. Triangulating the findings with key informants, plus checking and double-checking the data, can lessen the risk of fabricating it.

By planning, making sure they understand the assignment, keeping good notes, and doing drafts, students can reduce their chances of making serious attribution mistakes.

## Summarizing, Paraphrasing, and Quoting Sources

Anthropologists need to know how to summarize, paraphrase, and quote because they typically use all three techniques in any one paper. If you tend to rely exclusively on directly quoting, you need to widen your repertoire. Indeed, you'll need to make strategic decisions about when to use each of these three techniques. Paraphrasing is probably the most common among practicing researchers, but for students it is the most difficult to master. *All three always require an in-text citation.*

## Summarizing

Summarize when you are reducing large amounts of information (often a whole article or book) into overviews. Summaries are great for the first paragraphs of papers (although they can appear anywhere). You can introduce the works you plan to discuss in more detail later; such summaries often also set up the necessary background for introducing your thesis. The best summaries identify the most important points of the original work and usually retain the order of the original work's sequence of events. Summaries can be as brief as one sentence and as long as one paragraph.

Below are beginnings of two student essays on the ethnography *Guests of the Sheik* (Fernea 1989). Since the ethnography is a narrative, it makes sense to *retell* the story as a prelude to the student's own analysis.

......................................................................................................................................

Here is the original summary:

> *Guests of the Sheik* is an ethnography written by Elizabeth Fernea, chronicling her time spent living in El Nahra, an Iraqi village. Fernea lived there with her husband Bob, a social anthropologist, who was conducting research on the tribe. Elizabeth was the first Western woman to have lived in the strict Shiite village, and her husband believed it would be a great experience for her to gain insight into the different lifestyle of the women of El Nahra.

←— Contents: The writer mentions the title, author, and setting—although most of the details are written from the perspective of what Fernea's husband is doing rather than what she, the main character, is experiencing.

Here is a better summary:

> In the ethnography entitled *Guests of the Sheik* by Elizabeth Warnock Fernea, Fernea shares with the readers her experiences during a two-year period of her life in which she lived in a small Iraqi

village named El Nahra. Elizabeth, also
known as BJ, lives in this village along
with her husband Bob, who is works as
an anthropologist within the community.
Although BJ is not trained to be an anthropologist, her husband encourages
her to gather as much information as
possible about this female community in
which purdah is practiced. Through the
use of participant observation and an
immense amount of note taking,
BJ discovers what it is like to be a woman
in this patrilineal and patrifocal society.
As BJ transforms her life into one of a
traditional woman living in El Nahra, she
finally gains acceptance within their
community and finds an understanding
for this particular female culture.

← Contents: The writer
mentions the title,
author, and setting and
gives details about the
main characters, major
plot details, conflict,
and resolution. Here,
the focus is appropri-
ately placed on "BJ"
since she is telling the
story. Also note that the
student is incorporating
anthro terms and Iraqi
terms such as *purdah*.

## Paraphrasing

Paraphrase when you intend to restate the details of someone's
idea in your own words. Here's the tricky part: Paraphrasing
requires you to use not just your own words but also your own
*sentence structures.* Some students run into trouble when they
attempt paraphrasing because they:

- use exact, whole sentences or phrases from the original text
  without *quoting*
- use phrases from the original text without *citing*, even if
  much of the original text around it is rewritten
- mimic the syntax, structures, and examples of the original
  text.

It is *never* appropriate simply to change several words (or
even half of the words) in the original text and insert that into
your text. You can't do that even if you include a citation, but it
even more egregious if you omit a citation.

This passage is from "The Anthropologists in *Avatar*" by James W. Dow (2012, 30) from the book *The Heroic Anthropologist Rides Again: The Depiction of the Anthropologist in Popular Culture* (Salamone 2012):

> Where do the anthropologists in *Avatar* fit into the heroic imagery? My opinion is that they are more hero facilitators than action heroes themselves. Their strong adherence to scientific and humanistic values in telling the true story of the Na'vi draws them into the fight, but then they only fight alongside of the big action hero, Jake, who is motivated more by love and fury against those who are harming his girlfriend's family. The anthropologists see the justice of the fight and help it along, but they are not filled with the same outrage and determination as the hero. In some ways they are nobler than the action hero. They fight for scientific truth and the value of humanoid, animal, and plant life. They are sub-heroes. This is not so bad. Perhaps it is better to be a sub-hero and faithful to one's calling than an American hero of Hollywood proportions whose faithfulness to reality is only mythical.

Below are some examples of plagiarized text of the Dow article, followed by a correct paraphrase of the excerpt.

This first paraphrase violates academic norms because it uses exact sentences and phrases from the original text, even though it adds some text and swaps in a few synonyms. Also, there is no citation:

> Where do the anthropologists in *Avatar* fit into the heroic imagery? The anthropologists are more hero facilitators than action heroes themselves. Their strong adherence to scientific and humanistic values in telling the true story of the Na'vi draws them into the battle. They only fight alongside of

the big action hero, Jake, who is motivated more by love and fury against those who are hurting his girlfriend's family. The anthropologists see the justice of the fight and help it along, but they are not filled with the same anger and determination as the hero. In some ways they are nobler than the action hero. They fight for scientific truth and the value of humans, animals, and plants. They are sub-heroes.

This second paraphrase violates academic norms because it uses selected phrases and syntax from the original text, even if some of the original text around those phrases is rewritten. Also, the citation is missing:

The anthropologists in *Avatar* are more hero facilitators than action heroes. Their strong adherence to scientific and humanistic values brings them into the fight, but then they fight alongside Jake the hero, who is motivated more by love and fury against the mining company. The anthropologists see the justice of the fight but do not have the same justifications of the big action hero.

In contrast, here's an example of a decent paraphrase:

Dow (2011) believes that the anthropologists in the film *Avatar* are not the main heroes of the story but are ancillary heroes. The hero is motivated by love; in contrast, the anthropologists are motivated by their values and the injustices they see happening to the Na'vi people. Dow thinks that it is better to be motivated by philosophical commitments than by passion.

Remember that ultimately a good paraphrase is about grafting sources as organically as possible into your own argument. You not only compress selected parts of the source to

**A good paraphrase does the following:**

- Uses your own sentence structure
- Differentiates between your ideas and the author's ideas
- Includes a citation, properly placed.

make them handy as evidence but you also bring the style and syntax of the original closer to your own style, which makes for smoother (albeit clearly signaled and attributed) toggling between your ideas and those of your sources.

Where should you place the in-text citation? I've heard students say that if they are proud of a sentence they've crafted, and it includes a reference, they do not want it to look like the entire thought is being attributed to the reference. The solution is to know *where* to place the in-text citation. You have several options:

| Rule | Example |
|---|---|
| If the reference is at the beginning of the sentence, what follows is assumed to be your paraphrasing from the source. | Brown (2008) found that building rapport is central to cultural anthropology. |
| The same applies if the reference appears at the end. | Building rapport is central to cultural anthropology (Brown 2008). |
| If the reference is attached to only part of the sentence, then put the reference immediately after those words and use commas to distinguish between your words and the citation. | Building rapport is central to cultural anthropology (Brown 2008), but some anthropologists are better at it than others. |

## Quoting

Direct quotation is common in the humanities but rare in the sciences. In anthropology, directly quoting tends to be more common than in most other social sciences because the guideline is to quote only when an author's point of view is best said using his or her own words (Hubbuch 1992), and anthropologists put a premium on capturing other points of view.

Here's an excerpt from an introductory paragraph of a student's essay on *Guests of the Sheik* where BJ, an American woman, accompanies her new husband to a fundamentalist Muslim Egyptian village to finish his dissertation research. This student aims to point out that BJ initially protests but ends up immersing herself into the culture:

> When talking with her husband in Basra before traveling to El Nahra, B.J. had a particularly negative view of the abayahs or black veils that women were required to wear in Shiite tribal culture, remarking, "Why should I have to wear that ugly thing? It is not my custom" (Fernea 1965, 5). However, when she refused to wear the abayah people began to stare and point at her and she quickly put one on to bury herself within its anonymity.

This passage has a great setup: The preceding sentence gives you a specific picture of who's saying the quote and in what context. The student also takes the time to define "abayah" for the readers, which not only considers the audience's needs but also guards against alienating them with terms they might not know. Then, he connects the quote to his lead-in sentence. The quote is effective because it conveys BJ's revulsion of wearing this covering and her particular voice. The sentence immediately afterward provides the consequence, which creates a neat before-and-after effect.

Footnotes? No, anthropologists rarely use footnotes. The convention is that the writing you want your readers to see should be in the main text.

Quote when borrowing a key term from a source. If you look at journal articles written by anthropologists, they typically quote very short passages two or three times in the introduction, usually a phrase used by another writer, but not something much longer than that. For example, Kent, Santos, and Wade (2014) use quotations for the terminology of concepts coined by other researchers in the introduction of an article on genetic testing to determine ancestry in Brazil. Referencing a project that the BBC created to genetically test Brazilian celebrities, the authors put quotes around "Afro-Brazilian roots" and cite the source; because they want to further use the key term "imagined genetic communities," which was coined by another researcher (Simpson 2000), they likewise quote it, define it in their own words, and include a citation to Simpson.

Quote an informant/participant whose words best illustrate the point or support your claims. When you quote informants/participants in your research, you want their voice to come across in your writing, so quoting is frequent in qualitative research. Quotes are usually the end product of the analysis, so they're very important; Ladner (2014) considers them "currency." In case you haven't already noticed, people do not talk in complete, well-crafted sentences when they speak. If you are working with someone whose mastery of the language is not the best, the speech often ends up being broken. For your report, you may need to remove or add words, without changing the original thought or sentiment, so that the text is smooth for the reader. Use an ellipsis (. . .) to remove extraneous words or phrases as long as they do not change the meaning. Use brackets [ ] to indicate that you have added or changed certain words in minor ways.

  Indent any quote that is more than four lines long. Burnard (2004) points out that the use of longer quotes can be good for providing important context. When a quote runs longer than four lines, use a block quote—that is, indent the whole passage *and remove the quotation marks*. Use block quotes sparingly, though, because you do not want to look as if you are padding the paper with big quotes just to extend the page length. Use parentheses for the citation at the end of the block and put the period before the citation. In most circumstances, you wouldn't need to change a quotation, but if you opt to add italics as a special effect, you must note it in the following way:

> Credibility variables concentrate on how believable the work appears and focus on the researcher's qualifications and ability to undertake and accurately present the study. The answers to these questions are important when critiquing a piece of research as they can offer the reader *an insight into what to expect* in the remainder of the study. However, the reader should be aware that identified strengths and limitations within this section will not necessarily correspond with what will be found in the rest of the work. (Coughlan, et al. 2007: 658, emphasis added)

  Use a lead-in phrase or sentence to introduce a speaker or a published source. Some students have difficulty understanding how to quote from published sources, especially if the excerpt is an entire sentence. Students often choose the sentence they want, drop it into one of their paragraphs, add the page number and quotation marks at the beginning and end of the sentence, and (incorrectly) think that this is correct way to quote. Remember, quotations cannot stand alone. When you quote, you are incorporating someone else's words into your own prose. Therefore, you need both to create some distance between your words and someone else's (so that it is clear who's saying what) and to build a bridge between the your text and the quotation. The easiest way to do this is with *lead-in phrases* (also called *signal phrases*). For example:

As Alverez (2011) suggests, "..."

In contrast, Johnson (2013) argues, "..."

This is further supported by US Census data from 2010, which Riley (2015) has interpreted this way: "..."

In his interview, Mr. Chiu, Director of Development for the JRC, commented that he sees the agencies mission differently: "..."

If you use the author's name in your lead-in phrase or sentence, then you can omit it in the reference. Let's say you are citing from the book *Medical Anthropology and the World System* by Hans A. Baer, Merrill Singer, and Ida Susser (2003). You would write:

This concept is described by Baer et al. (2004) as critical of the role of capitalism in healthcare.

Note that since "Baer et al." is in your sentence, it doesn't need to be repeated inside the parentheses. You could also cite specific page numbers or page ranges:

(Baer, Singer, and Susser 2003, 126) or (Baer, Singer, and Susser 2003, 120–132).

Lead-in phrases announce, "Hey, I'm about to use some borrowed information." Think of yourself as a reporter interviewing someone with a microphone in your hand. You say a few sentences and then point the mic at your interviewee, who says what she wants to say, and then you return the microphone to yourself to explain and summarize what the person just said.

Verbs are central to lead-in phrases, and the most common ones we see are *states, writes*, and *argues*. But the more precise you can be with your verbs, the better. The right verb helps your readers better grasp both the original intent of the author you are quoting and the purpose that you intend a given direct quotation to serve in your own argument. Here are some handy verbs for lead-in phrases:

| | | | |
|---|---|---|---|
| acknowledges | adds | admits | affirms |
| agrees | answers | argues | asks |
| asserts | attacks | believes | calls |
| claims | comments | compares | concedes |
| confirms | contends | counters | counterattacks |
| declares | defines | denies | disputes |
| echoes | emphasizes | endorses | estimates |
| finds | grants | illustrates | implies |
| insinuates | insists | labels | mentions |
| notes | observes | points out | predicts |
| proposes | reasons | recognizes | recommends |
| refutes | rejects | reports | responds |
| retorts | reveals | says | speculates |
| states | suggests | surmises | tells |
| thinks | warns | writes | |

(*Source*: Hacker, Cohen, Sussman, and Villar-Smith 2007)

Another sound strategy is to follow each quote with at least one sentence that explains it. You might also remark on how it

## Verb Tenses and Quoted Material

When introducing a *published* source, use the present tense:

> In contrast, Johnson (2013) <u>argues</u> . . .
> Hacker (2007) <u>lists</u> a range of possible verbs to use to introduce source material.

When using a lead-in phrase to introduce *interview* material, use the past tense (see the student example).

contributes to your ongoing argument. In this way, you are building your own authority.

Here is a good example of three ways to incorporate a quote into sentences (shown highlighted). For this assignment, students wrote a report on research consisting of one-on-one qualitative interviews on school spirit that they conducted with other students.

........................................................................................................................

Another topic which also evoked variance in opinions was whether students believed that living on or off campus influenced school spirit. The students who had lived on campus during all their academic careers did not consider the place of residence to impact the amount of school spirit. They often stressed that as long as students wanted to be involved on campus, they could make it happen. On the other hand, students who had lived both on and off campus described elaborately the distinction between the two residence patterns, as well as how

← "Variance" is a statistical term that doesn't really belong here. "Variety" is more appropriate.

distance from campus might diminish school spirit or at least involvement. Chris, a transportation and urban planning major, spoke about this matter with expertise from his personal experience and his field of study:

> When you are on campus, you are living on campus, you are breathing on campus, you are doing everything on campus and, especially with everyone so close together in a situation, that's where community is drawn from . . . And that interaction really builds up good community. And when you have a good community, then you have good pride.

For Chris, community and school pride were interrelated. He proceeded to share that his life off campus had reduced his sense of community and consequently his school pride. Other students also shared Chris' experience of diminished school spirit (hence pride) because of living far from the campus. The majority, if not all the respondents associated interest in sports with school spirit. Likewise, the lack of sports enthusiasm was often acknowledged as lack of school spirit. Because of this limiting widespread definition of school spirit, some students originally reported not being school-spirited. For instance, one of the students—the 20-year-old Nicole—initially denied having any school spirit. Nevertheless, throughout the interview Nicole came to realize that she had school spirit but it was not "in the generic, stereotypical way through sports."

There was some disagreement about the role of academics in fostering school pride and spirit. The interviews revealed that many students today considered school pride to be associated solely with sports,

Method #1: A lead-in sentence orients the reader to what follows, including the speaker of the direct quotation. Notice how a colon at the end of the lead-in sentence signals to readers, "here comes what I was just introducing."

Immediately after the quotation, the student summarizes the person's statement. This reinforces the sentiment for the reader.

Method #2: The quotation is directly integrated into a sentence. You might need to change the verb or subject slightly to fit your sentence, but don't change the context— that would be misrepresentation.

excluding academics. Very few students indicated academics as a source of pride, especially personal pride of achievement rather than institutional collective pride. For instance during interviews, Nicole did ←— recognize school pride as both academic and athletic pride while Eli stated, "I feel like academics do not have anything to do with school spirit."

Method #3: A verb like "to state" is followed by a comma and the entire quote attributed to the person. With this method you don't have to fit the quote into your sentence, but it also reads a little "journalistic." The reader can get tired of this method if you use it too frequently.

This student shows competence in quoting interviewees. In the first paragraph she employs a block quote preceded by a colon because it is an extended response, in this case three sentences. The author wanted to make it clear that these words were not her own. In the second paragraph she connects a phrase from an interviewee to her own words in the sentence. In the third paragraph she uses a comma to set apart an entire sentence quoted from an interviewee. All three ways are very effective options for introducing a quotation from an interview. If you plan to quote often, try not to overuse one sentence format. Instead, do as this student did and vary the ways that you introduce quotations and incorporate them into your own sentences.

## AAA/Chicago Style Source Documentation

Every source that you use must include (1) an in-text parenthetical citation and (2) a corresponding reference list entry.

### In-Text Parenthetical Citations

Place the parenthetical in-text citation at the end of the sentence, passage, or phrase you are attributing to the author, whether you are directly quoting, paraphrasing, or summarizing. When summarizing a whole work, do not include page numbers; when directly quoting or paraphrasing, include the page number or a page range. This same format is used for books, book chapters, journal articles, newspaper articles, popular magazine articles, photographs, dissertations, or unpublished interviews.

There are two main ways to place the in-text citation—at the end of the passage or directly after introducing the author of the source:

> Others have argued that poststructuralism had a negative effect on the field (Moore 1994).

> In his award-winning essay, David Chioni Moore (1994) argues that anthropology has always had two modes, scientific and interpretive, but that the poststructuralism that swept the field in the 1980s caused anthropology to "lose its nerve" (346).

Note that in the second case, a page number is included. If Moore had not been mentioned in the lead-in phrase, that page number would have been included in the in-text citation at the end of the sentence: (Moore 1994, 346).

## Special Cases

For an in-text citation of a work with three or more authors, use "et al.," but write all of their names for the reference.

> (Baer et al. 2003)

> This concept is described by Baer et al. (2003) as . . .

For multiple references by the same author published in the same year, distinguish the references by letter:

> (Rapp 1993a) and (Rapp 1993b) or (Rapp 1993a; Rapp 1993b)

## Websites

Citing website or blog content can often be limited to a mention in the text:

> As of March 10, 2016, Google's privacy policy . . .
> The following passages can be found on the Writers on Writing section of Durham University's Writing Across Boundaries website: . . .

If a more formal in-text citation is desired, it may be styled as, in the first example, (Google 2016). See the *References List* section below for how to create a corresponding reference entry for each website.

For multiple references by the same author published in different years, use this style:

(Rapp 1993) and (Rapp 1997) or (Rapp 1993; Rapp 1997)

For two works by two different authors in the same sentence, order them alphabetically by author, regardless of date published, and separate them with semicolons:

(Clifford 1988; Rapp 1993)

Original interviews that you collected do not require in-text citations or reference entries because they are considered raw data.

## References List

If a source is in your list of references at the end, there must be an in-text citation for it in the body of your paper, and vice versa. On the other hand, a bibliography is a broader list, a list of sources you used while creating the work but did not necessarily cite.

Depending on how you work, you might choose to insert the in-text citations as you write the sections of your paper and then take a few hours to create the list of references. An alternative is to insert the citations and do the references as you write, which guards against accidentally omitting a reference at the end of the paper.

Most anthropologists now use bibliographic citation software in two ways: (1) to export the sources they want to use from research databases into a personalized reference library and (2) to cite the sources simultaneously in the text of the paper and at the end as a reference. Using such programs as Endnote, RefWorks, and Zotero saves a lot of time and helps you keep orderly records. But some words of caution: You still have to check (and double-check) each source you cite or download.

Here are styles for various types of publications. Because a brief guide cannot cover every source documentation issue, you can consult the latest edition of *The Chicago Manual of Style* for any circumstances not addressed in this chapter.

## Capitalization of Words in Titles

Chicago style is not particular about whether you should use the *sentence case* or the *title case*. In sentence case, only the first word is capitalized. In title case, most of the words—all the important ones—are capitalized.

No matter which style you choose, be consistent. The examples presented here show both types so that you can see the differences between them.

### 1. Book, single author

Author's last name, first name. Year. *Title*. Publication Place: Publisher.

Baer, Hans. 2004. *Toward an Integrative Medicine: Merging Alternative Therapies with Biomedicine*. Walnut Creek, CA: AltaMira Press.

### 2. Book, multiple authors

First author's last name, first name; second author's first name last name. Year. *Title*. Publication Place: Publisher.

Baer, Hans A., Merrill Singer, and Ida Susser. 2003. *Medical Anthropology and the World System*. Westport, CT: Praeger.

### 3. Book chapter

Chapter author's last name, first name. Year. "Title of Chapter." In *Title of Book*, edited by editor's first name last name, page numbers xxx–xxx. Publication Place: Publisher.

Calvin, William H. 2001. "Pumping Up Intelligence: Abrupt Climate Jumps and the Evolution of Higher Intellectual Functions During the Ice Ages." In *The Evolution of Intelligence*, edited by Robert J. Sternberg and James C. Kaufman, 97–115. Mahwah, NJ: Lawrence Erlbaum Associates.

Clifford, James. 1988. "Identity in Mashpee." In *The Predicament of Culture*, edited by James Clifford, 277–348. Cambridge, MA: Harvard University Press.

### 4. Multiple references by the same author published in different years

Order chronologically.

Rapp, Rayna. 1993. "Sociocultural differences in the impact of amniocentesis: an anthropological research report." *Fetal Diagnosis and Therapy* 8(Suppl. 1):90–96.

Rapp, Rayna. 1997. "Communicating about chromosomes: patients, providers, and cultural assumptions." *Journal of the American Medical Women's Association* no. 52(1):28–9, 32.

Note: The Rapp 1997 article has non-consecutive page numbers; it spans page 28 and 29 of the journal, skips a few pages and concludes on page 32.

**5. Multiple references by the same author published in the same year**
Order alphabetically by article title. Note: The author or set of authors must be *exactly* the same for this style to apply.

Rapp, Rayna. 1993a. "Amniocentesis in sociocultural perspective." *Journal of Genetic Counseling* 2(3):183–196. doi:10.1007/BF00962079.

Rapp, Rayna. 1993b. "Sociocultural differences in the impact of amniocentesis: an anthropological research report." *Fetal Diagnosis and Therapy* 8(Suppl. 1):90–96. doi:10.1159/000263877.

A common issue is how to provide a reference for journal articles found online using a database instead of as a physical volume on a shelf. *The Chicago Manual of Style* suggests using the same format for printed periodicals but adding the Digital Object Identifier (DOI) or URL. The DOI is a unique, permanent number assigned to documents and online content so that if they move to other websites, they can still be found. If the DOI is not present for your journal article, then use the URL. The database JSTOR, for example, provides both; the "stable URL" for each journal article is located on JSTOR's webpages near the other publishing information you would use to create the reference. The accessed date (the date you accessed the database) is not necessary, but if you choose to add an accessed date, separate the date by a period.

**6. Article in journal, newspaper, or popular magazine**
Author's last name, first name. Year. "Title of Article." *Title of Journal* Volume(Issue):page numbers of the entire article. doi:number.

Hsu, Francis L. K. 1964. "Rethinking the concept 'primitive'." *Current Anthropology* 5(3):169–178. doi:10.2307/2740177.

**7. Article from a Website**
Author's last name, first name. Year. "Title of Article." *Title of Journal*, Volume(Issue) or Issue date. Accessed date. URL.

Kolbert, Elizabeth. 2013. "Modern Life—Up All Night: The Science of Sleeplessness." *The New Yorker*, March 11. Accessed February 12, 2014. http://www.newyorker.com/reporting/2013/03/11/130311fa_fact_kolbert.

If there is no author, begin the citation with the article title.

**8. Websites**
Site author (can be the name of an organization or the author's last name, first name). Year. "Title of Site." Last modified date (if available). Accessed date. URL.

Philadelphia Museum of Art. 2014. "Research: Conservation." Accessed February 12, 2014. http://www.philamuseum.org/conservation/.

# GUIDE TO PEER REVIEW IN ANTHROPOLOGY

Peer review can be an efficient way to receive feedback on writing during those difficult intermediate stages. If you take the process seriously, you'll acquire the following skills:

- Learn to give constructive criticism to another student writer
- Learn to receive feedback on your own work
- Develop your ability to pay attention to detail

Even the best professional writers need editors who provide thoughtful feedback throughout the writing process. Peer review is a kind of editing, but keep in mind that it is *not* copyediting. Peer review works best when you focus on "higher-order" concerns like the quality of analysis and evidence *before* moving on to sentence-level copyediting. Here is one experience-tested way to navigate the process:

1. Ask the writer to identify things that he or she wants you to look for in the paper. The writer can write this in at the top of the draft—something like, "What I would like you to pay particular attention to is . . ." or "What I especially need help with is my conclusion/making it longer/integrating sources/etc."

2. Provide the writer with a summary of what you believe the paper is about. Be sure to include what you believe the main idea is.

3. Phrase your responses to the writer as "I" statements—rather than telling the writer what to do, give him or her a sense of what you are *experiencing* as a reader. The writer's job is then to figure out what to do. Examples: "When I read this, I hear . . .," "I'm confused by this section here . . .," "I'm interested in seeing more expansion of this thought . . ."

4. Attend first to the broad, higher-order concerns.

- What is the main idea? Is it clear? Does the argument make a plausible claim?
- What do you think is the *strongest* part of the draft? Which other specific parts seem especially insightful or promising?
- Is there enough evidence? The right kinds of evidence?
- Can you follow the line of development? Are the sections arranged in optimal order?
- Do any parts seem extraneous or puzzling?

5. Look for anthropology-specific issues in the writing.

To what extent does the paper reflect cultural relativism, context/history, description, reflexivity? (any anthropology assignment)

Does the writer appear to pay special attention to writing about race, ethnicity, gender, and special populations? (any Anthropology assignment)

To what extent does the paper evaluate the strengths and weaknesses of the source(s)? (critiques, literature review)

To what extent does the writer seem to connect to the source? If so, is the way that the writer is connecting to the source clear? (reader response)

To what extent does the writer use appropriate words that reflect the writer's emotion, the tone of the source material, and the quality of the text? (reader response)

To what extent does the writer put the book or film being reviewed in its appropriate context? (book/film review)

To what extent does the writer evaluate the strengths and weaknesses of the book or film? (book/film review)

To what extent does the book/film review identify underlying assumptions, distinctive features, implications, or something otherwise interesting about the work? (book/film review)

How well does the writer describe the field experience? (field-based assignment)

To what extent is the writer being reflexive? (field-based assignment)

How clearly is the ethnographic data arranged? (field-based assignment)

How well-defined is the topic? Too broad, narrow, too unwieldy? (literature review, any research article)

To what extent does the writer identify relationships and patterns between the sources? (literature review, any research article)

Does the introduction clearly announce the topic and explain its significance? (any research article)

Does the introduction provide an overview of prior research? (any research article)

Does the introduction include a statement of the problem? (any research article)

Does the introduction explain how the present work builds on previous research? (any research article)

Does the author signal which move is occurring at each point? (any research article)

How well are the research findings represented by tables and graphs? (any research article)

To what extent does the discussion summarize the findings, identify the strengths and limitations of the study, and describe any implications for future research? (any research article)

To what extent does the abstract summarize the research? (any research article)

6. Does the writer use appropriate citations, quoting, and paraphrasing?

7. If the draft you are reviewing is an early draft, you probably shouldn't focus on sentence-level concerns. But if it is a later draft, comment on which sentence-level concerns you see *most frequently* causing trouble. Name the top three issues that the writer should focus on correcting.

| | |
|---|---|
| Spelling | Subject–verb agreement |
| Pronouns | Redundant words |
| Sentence fragments and run-on sentences | Active/passive voice |
| Articles (a/an/the/zero article) | Capitalization |
| Parallel sentence structure | Transition words (too many, too few, or not the right ones) |
| Punctuation | Wordiness |

8. End with either two *questions* for the writer or two *suggestions* for revising.

# REFERENCES

Agar, Michael. 1980. *The Professional Stranger: An Informal Introduction to Ethnography, Studies in Anthropology*. New York: Academic Press.

Anderson, Leon. 2006. "Analytic autoethnography." *Journal of Contemporary Ethnography* 35(4):373–395. doi:10.1177/0891241605280449.

Arnold, Lynnette. 2012. "Reproducing actions, reproducing power: local ideologies and everyday practices of participation at a California community bike shop." *Journal of Linguistic Anthropology* 22(3): 137–158. doi:10.1111/j.1548-1395.2012.01153.x.

Baer, Hans A., Merrill Singer, and Ida Susser. 2003. *Medical Anthropology and the World System*. 2nd ed. Westport, CT: Praeger.

Beck, Sam, and Carl A. Maida. 2013. *Toward Engaged Anthropology*. New York: Berghahn Books.

Berrett, Lorna. 2016. *Optimizing Your Article for Search Engines*. John Wiley & Sons. Available from https://authorservices.wiley.com/bauthor/seo.asp [Accessed March 4, 2016].

Bessire, Lucas, and David Bond. 2014. "Ontological anthropology and the deferral of critique." *American Ethnologist* 41(3):440–456. doi:10.1111/amet.12083.

Blommaert, Jan, and Dong Jie. 2010. *Ethnographic Fieldwork: A Beginner's Guide*. Bristol: Multilingual Matters.

Boeri, M. W., D. Gibson, and L. Harbry. 2009. "Cold cook methods: an ethnographic exploration on the myths of methamphetamine production and policy implications." *International Journal of Drug Policy* 20(5):438–443.

Bonanno, Alessandro, and Douglas H. Constance. 2001. "Globalization, Fordism, and post-Fordism in agriculture and food: a critical review of the literature." *Culture & Agriculture* 23(2):1–18. doi:10.1525/cag.2001.23.2.1.

Booth, Wayne C., Gregory G. Colomb, and Joseph M. Williams. 1995. *The Craft of Research*. Chicago: University of Chicago Press.

Brezina, Vaclav. 2013. "Philosophical Anthropology and Philosophy in Anthropology." In *Philosophy and Anthropology: Border Crossing and*

*Transformations,* edited by Ananta Kumar Giri and J. R. Clammer. New York: Anthem Press.

Brooks, Peter, and Hilary Jewett. 2014. *The Humanities and Public Life.* New York: Fordham University Press.

Bryan, Andy. 2006. "Back from yet another globetrotting adventure, Indiana Jones checks his mail and discovers that his bid for tenure has been denied." *McSweeney's,* October 11. [Accessed January 17, 2013.] http://www.mcsweeneys.net/articles/back-from-yet-another -globetrotting-adventure-indiana-jones-checks-his-mail-and -discovers-that-his-bid-for-tenure-has-been-denied.

Bryant, Rebecca. 2014. "History's remainders: on time and objects after conflict in cyprus." *American Ethnologist* 41(4):681–697. doi:10.1111 /amet.12105.

Burnard, Philip. 2004. "Writing a qualitative research report." *Nurse Education Today* 24(3):174–179. doi:http://dx.doi.org/10.1016/j .nedt.2003.11.005.

Carli, Linda L. 1990. "Gender, language, and influence." *Journal of Personality and Social Psychology* 59(5):941–951. doi:10.1037 /0022-3514.59.5.941.

Chalk, Janine, Barth W. Wright, Peter W. Lucas, Katherine D. Schuhmacher, Erin R. Vogel, Dorothy Fragaszy, Elisabetta Visalberghi, Patrícia Izar, and Brian G. Richmond. 2016. "Age-related variation in the mechanical properties of foods processed by Sapajus libidinosus." *American Journal of Physical Anthropology* 159(2):199–209. doi:10.1002/ajpa.22865.

Clifford, James, and George E. Marcus. 1986. *Writing Culture: The Poetics and Politics of Ethnography.* Berkeley: University of California.

Constable, Nicole. 2003. *Romance on a Global Stage: Pen Pals, Virtual Ethnography, and "Mail-Order" Marriages.* Berkeley: University of California Press.

Cooper, Harris M., and American Psychological Association. 2011. *Reporting Research in Psychology: How to Meet Journal Article Reporting Standards.* Washington, DC: American Psychological Association.

Davies, Charlotte Aull. 1999. *Reflexive Ethnography: A Guide to Researching Selves and Pthers.* London; New York: Routledge.

De Brigard, Emilie. 2003. "The History of Ethnographic Film." In *Principles of Visual Anthropology*, edited by Paul Edward Hockings. Berlin; New York: Mouton de Gruyter.

Dow, James W. 2012. "The Anthropologists in *Avatar*." In *The Heroic Anthropologist Rides Again: The Depiction of the Anthropologist in Popular Culture*, edited by Frank A. Salamone. Newcastle: Cambridge Scholars Publishing.

Ellis, Stephen. 2006. "Witchcraft, violence, and democracy in South Africa." American Anthropologist 108 (2):401-401. doi: 10.1525 /aa.2006.108.2.401.

Emerson, Robert M., Rachel I. Fretz, and Linda L. Shaw. 1995. *Writing Ethnographic Fieldnotes, Chicago Guides to Writing, Editing, and Publishing*. Chicago: University of Chicago Press.

Fernea, Elizabeth Warnock. 1989. *Guests of the Sheik: An Ethnography of an Iraqi Village*. New York: Doubleday.

First Nations Studies Program, University of British Columbia. 2009. *Identity: Terminology*. Available from http://indigenousfoundations.arts .ubc.ca/home/identity/terminology.html [Accessed March 4, 2016].

Geertz, Clifford. 1973. "Thick description: toward an interpretive theory of culture." In *The Interpretation of Cultures: Selected Essays*. New York: Basic Books.

Gorden, Raymond L. 1992. *Basic Interviewing Skills*. Itasca, IL: F.E. Peacock.

Grinker, Roy Richard. 2000. *In the Arms of Africa: The Life of Colin M. Turnbull*. New York: St. Martin's Press.

Hacker, Diana, Samuel Cohen, Barbara D. Sussman, and Maria Villar-Smith. 2007. *Rules for Writers*. 5th ed. Boston; New York: Bedford/St. Martin's.

Hannig, Anita. 2015. "Sick healers: chronic affliction and the authority of experience at an ethiopian hospital." *American Anthropologist* 117(4):640–651. doi:10.1111/aman.12337.

Harris, Joseph. 2006. *Rewriting: How to Do Things with Texts*. Logan: Utah State University Press.

Harris, Marvin. 1992. "The cultural ecology of India's sacred cattle." *Current Anthropology* 33(1):261–276. doi:10.2307/2743946.

Heider, Karl G. 2007. *Ethnographic Film*. Austin: University of Texas Press.

Herzfeld, Michael. 2010. "Essentialism." In *Routledge Encyclopedia of Social and Cultural Anthropology*, edited by Alan Barnard and Jonathan Spencer. London: Routledge.

Hubbuch, Susan M. 1992. *Writing Research Papers Across the Curriculum*. Fort Worth, TX: Harcourt Brace Jovanovich.

Isbell, Billie Jean. 2009. *Finding Cholita*. Urbana: University of Illinois Press.

JAMA Internal Medicine. 2016 (February 11). *JAMA Internal Medicine Instructions for Authors*. Available from http://archinte.jamanetwork.com/public/instructionsForAuthors.aspx [Accessed March 4, 2016].

Johnson Jr,, William A., Richard P. Rettig, Gregory M. Scott, and Stephen M. Garrison. 2004. *The Sociology Student Writer's Manual*. Upper Saddle River, NJ: Pearson Education.

Kaprow, Miriam Lee. 1985. "Manufacturing danger: fear and pollution in industrial society." *American Anthropologist* 87(2):342–356. doi:10.1525/aa.1985.87.2.02a00070.

Kent, Michael, Ricardo Ventura Santos, and Peter Wade. 2014. "Negotiating imagined genetic communities: unity and diversity in Brazilian science and society." *American Anthropologist* 116(4):736–748. doi:10.1111/aman.12142.

Khazaleh, Lorenz. 2007. "Anthropologists condemn the use of terms of 'Stone Age' and 'primitive'." In *antropologi.info*, edited by Lorenz Khazaleh.

Ladner, Sam. 2014. *Practical Ethnography: A Guide to Doing Ethnography in the Private Sector*. Walnut Creek, CA: Left Coast Press.

Laterza, Vito. 2007. "The ethnographic novel: another literary skeleton in the anthropological closet?" *Suomen Anthropologi: Journal of the Finnish Anthropological Society* 32(2):124–134.

Lee, Richard Borshay. 2007. "Eating Christmas in the Kalahari." In *Annual Editions: Anthropology 07/08*, edited by Elvio Angeloni. Guilford, CT: Dushkin Publishing Group.

Lélé, Sharachchandra, and Richard B. Norgaard. 2005. "Practicing interdisciplinarity." *BioScience* 55(11):967–975. doi:10.1641/0006-3568(2005)055[0967:pi]2.0.co;2.

Lett, James William. 1987. *The Human Enterprise: A Critical Introduction to Anthropological Theory*. Boulder, CO: Westview Press.

Low, Setha M., and Sally Engle Merry. 2010. "Engaged anthropology: diversity and dilemmas: an introduction to supplement 2." *Current Anthropology* 51(S2):S203–S226. doi:10.1086/653837.

Marcus, George E. 2009. "Notes Toward an Ethnographic Memoir of Supervising Graduate Research Through Anthropology's Decades of Transformation." In *Fieldwork Is Not What It Used To Be: Learning Anthropology's Method in a Time of Transition*, edited by James D. Faubion and George E. Marcus. Ithaca, NY: Cornell University Press.

Marr, Bernard. 2014 (November 24). "People, please stop using pie charts." *Entrepreneur Magazine*. Available from http://www.entrepreneur.com/article/239932 [Accessed March 4, 2016].

Matthews, Janice R., and Robert W. Matthews. 2008. *Successful Scientific Writing: A Step-by-Step Guide for the Biological and Medical Sciences*. 3rd ed. Cambridge, UK; New York: Cambridge University Press.

McClaurin, Irma. 2001. *Black Feminist Anthropology: Theory, Politics, Praxis, and Poetics*. New Brunswick, NJ: Rutgers University Press.

McGill, Kenneth. 2013. "Political economy and language: a review of some recent literature." *Journal of Linguistic Anthropology* 23(2):E84–E101. doi:10.1111/jola.12015.

Moore, David Chioni. 1994. "Anthropology is dead, long live anthro(a) pology: poststructuralism, literary studies, and anthropology's 'nervous present'." *Journal of Anthropological Research* 50(4): 345–365. doi:10.2307/3630558.

Mukhopadhyay, Carol C., and Yolanda T. Moses. 1997. "Reestablishing 'race' in anthropological discourse." *American Anthropologist* 99(3):517–533. doi:10.1525/aa.1997.99.3.517.

Mulder, Monique Borgerhoff, T. M. Caro, James S. Chrisholm, Jean-Paul Dumont, Roberta L. Hall, Robert A. Hinde, and Ryutaro Ohtsuka. 1985. "The use of quantitative observational techniques in anthropology [and comments and replies]." *Current Anthropology* 26(3):323–335.

Narayan, Kirin. 1999. "Ethnography and fiction: where is the border?" *Anthropology and Humanism* 24(2):134–147. doi:10.1525/ahu.1999.24.2.134.

Narayan, Kirin. 2007. "Tools to shape texts: what creative nonfiction can offer ethnography." *Anthropology and Humanism* 32(2):130–144. doi:10.1525/ahu.2007.32.2.130.

National Cancer Institute—Office of Communications and Education. 2011. *Making Data Talk: A Workbook*. Bethesda, MD: U.S. Dept. of Health and Human Services, National Institutes of Health, National Cancer Institute.

National Park Service, U.S. Department of the Interior. 2016. *Ancestral Puebloans and Their World*. Available from http://www.nps.gov /meve/learn/education/upload/ancestral_puebloans.pdf [Accessed March 4, 2016].

Nelson, Margaret C., Scott E. Ingram, Andrew J. Dugmore, Richard Streeter, Matthew A. Peeples, Thomas H. McGovern, Michelle Hegmon, Jette Arneborg, Keith W. Kintigh, Seth Brewington, Katherine A. Spielmann, Ian A. Simpson, Colleen Strawhacker, Laura E. L. Comeau, Andrea Torvinen, Christian K. Madsen, George Hambrecht, and Konrad Smiarowski. 2016. "Climate challenges, vulnerabilities, and food security." *Proceedings of the National Academy of Sciences* 113(2):298–303. doi:10.1073/pnas.1506494113.

Pettigrew, Thomas F. 1996. *How to Think Like a Social Scientist*. New York: HarperCollins College Publishers.

Pillow, Wanda. 2003. "Confession, catharsis, or cure? Rethinking the uses of reflexivity as methodological power in qualitative research." *International Journal of Qualitative Studies in Education* 16(2): 175–196. doi: 10.1080/0951839032000060635.

Pyburn, K. Anne. 2008. "Shaken, not stirred: the revolution in archaeology." *Archeological Papers of the American Anthropological Association* 18(1):115–124. doi:10.1111/j.1551-8248.2008.00009.x.

Ramage, John D., and John C. Bean. 2000. *The Allyn and Bacon Guide to Writing*. Boston: Allyn and Bacon.

Roberts, David. 2015. *The Lost World of the Old Ones: Discoveries in the Ancient Southwest*. New York: W. W. Norton & Company.

Robertson, Jennifer. 2002. "Reflexivity redux: a pithy polemic on 'positionality'." *Anthropological Quarterly* 75(4):785–792.

Rosnow, Ralph L., and Mimi Rosnow. 2012. *Writing Papers in Psychology: A Student Guide*. 9th ed. Belmont, CA: Wadsworth Publishing.

Ruby, Jay. 1980. "Exposing yourself: reflexivity, anthropology, and film." *Semiotica* 30(1-2):153. doi:10.1515/semi.1980.30.1-2.153.

Salamone, Frank A. 2012. *The Heroic Anthropologist Rides Again: The Depiction of the Anthropologist in Popular Culture*. Newcastle: Cambridge Scholars Publishing.

Salzman, Philip Carl. 2002. "On reflexivity." *American Anthropologist* 104(3):805–811. doi:10.1525/aa.2002.104.3.805.

Schensul, Jean J., and Margaret Diane LeCompte. 1999. *Ethnographer's Toolkit*. Walnut Creek, CA: AltaMira Press.

Schmidt, Randell, Maureen Smyth, and Virginia Kowalski. 2014. *Teaching the Scientific Literature Review*. Santa Barbara, CA: ABC-CLIO.

Simpson, Bob. 2000. "Imagined genetic communities: ethnicity and essentialism in the twenty-first century." *Anthropology Today* 16(3):3–6. doi:10.1111/1467-8322.00023.

Smithsonian Museum of Natural History. 2016 (February 29). *Human Evolution Timeline Interactive*. Available from http://humanorigins .si.edu/evidence/human-evolution-timeline-interactive [Accessed March 1, 2016].

Smyth, T. Raymond. 2004. *The Principles of Writing in Psychology*. Houndmills: Palgrave Macmillan.

Society for American Archaeology. 2014. "Editorial policy, information for authors, and style guide for *American Antiquity, Latin American Antiquity* and *Advances in Archaeological Practice*." Available from http://www.saa.org/AbouttheSociety/Publications/StyleGuide /tabid/984/Default.aspx [accessed October 14, 2014].

Sterk, Claire E. 2000. *Tricking and Tripping: Prostitution in the Era of AIDS*. Putnam Valley, NY: Social Change Press.

Sternberg, Robert J. 1993. *The Psychologist's Companion: A Guide to Scientific Writing for Students and Researchers*. 3rd ed. Cambridge: Cambridge University Press.

Sullivan, Patrick. Writing With Your Head in Your Hands. Durham University Department of Anthropology, May 23, 2016 [Accessed December 12 2015]. Available from https://www.dur.ac.uk /writingacrossboundaries/writingonwriting/patricksullivan/.

Tedlock, Barbara, and Jane Kepp. 2005. "Some tips for better writing." *Anthropology News* 46(4):36–36. doi:10.1525/an.2005.46.4.36.1.

Tedlock, Dennis. 1999. "Poetry and ethnography: a dialogical approach." *Anthropology and Humanism* 24(2):155–167. doi:10.1525/ahu.1999 .24.2.155.

Tong, Allison, Peter Sainsbury, and Jonathan Craig. 2007. "Consolidated Criteria for Reporting Qualitative Research (COREQ): a 32-item checklist for interviews and focus groups." *International Journal for Quality in Health Care* 19(6):349–357. doi:10.1093/intqhc/mzm042.

Toulmin, Stephen. 1958. *The Uses of Argument*. Cambridge: Cambridge University Press.

Toulson, Ruth E. 2014. "Eating the food of the gods: interpretive dilemmas in anthropological analysis." *Anthropology and Humanism* 39(2):159–173. doi:10.1111/anhu.12053.

Turnbull, Colin M. 1961. *The Forest People*. New York: Simon and Schuster.

U.S. Census Bureau. 2013 (July 25). *Hispanic Origin*. Available from http://www.census.gov/topics/population/hispanic-origin/about .html [Accessed March 4, 2016].

University of Adelaide Writing Centre. 2014. *Writing an Abstract*. Available from https://www.adelaide.edu.au/writingcentre /learning_guides/learningGuide_writingAnAbstract.pdf [Accessed December 10, 2014].

Villarreal, Yazmin. 2015 (March 27). *Sweden Is Adding a Gender-Neutral Pronoun to Its Dictionary*. Available from http://www.advocate.com /world/2015/03/27/sweden-adding-gender-neutral-pronoun-its -dictionary [Accessedd March 4, 2016].

Vonnegut, Kurt. 1981. *Palm Sunday: An Autobiographical Collage*. New York: Delacorte Press.

Weida, Stacy, and Karl Stolley. 2014 (November 6). *Organizing Your Argument*. Purdue University Online Writing Lab. Available from https://owl.english.purdue.edu/owl/resource/588/03/ [Accessed March 4, 2016].

Williams, Drid. 2000. *Anthropology and Human Movement: Searching for Origins*. Lanham, MD: Scarecrow Press.

Williams, Joseph M. 1990. *Style: toward Clarity and Grace*. Chicago, IL: University of Chicago Press.

Wolcott, Harry F. 1995. *The Art of Fieldwork*. Walnut Creek, CA: AltaMira Press.

Wolcott, Harry F. 2010. *Ethnography Lessons: A Primer*. Walnut Creek, CA: Left Coast Press.

Writing Center, University of North Carolina at Chapel Hill. 2012. *Understanding Assignments*. Available from http://writingcenter .unc.edu/handouts/understanding-assignments/ [Accessed November 15, 2014].

# NOTES

## Chapter 1

1. Beck S, Maida CA, eds. Toward engaged anthropology. New York: Berghahn Books; 2013.
2. Vonnegut K. Palm sunday: an autobiographical collage. New York: Delacorte Press; 1981.
3. Lett JW. The human enterprise : a critical introduction to anthropological theory. Boulder: Westview Press; 1987.
4. Low Setha M, Merry Sally E. Engaged anthropology: diversity and dilemmas: an introduction to supplement 2. Current Anthropology 2010; 51:S203–S26.
5. Clifford J, Marcus GE. Writing culture: the poetics and politics of ethnography. Berkeley: University of California; 1986.
6. McClaurin I. Black feminist anthropology : theory, politics, praxis, and poetics. New Brunswick, NJ: Rutgers University Press; 2001.
7. Anderson L. Analytic autoethnography. Journal of Contemporary Ethnography 2006; 35:373–95.
8. Narayan K. Tools to shape texts: what creative nonfiction can offer ethnography. Anthropology and Humanism 2007; 32:130–44.
9. Tedlock D. Poetry and ethnography: a dialogical approach. Anthropology and Humanism 1999; 24:155–67.
10. Narayan K. Ethnography and fiction: where Is the border? Anthropology and Humanism 1999; 24:134–47.
11. Isbell BJ. Finding cholita. Urbana: University of Illinois Press; 2009.
12. Laterza V. The ethnographic novel: another literary skeleton in the anthropological closet? Suomen Anthropologi: Journal of the Finnish Anthropological Society 2007; 32:124–34.
13. Pettigrew TF. How to think like a social scientist. New York: HarperCollins College Publishers; 1996.
14. Davies CA. Reflexive ethnography : a guide to researching selves and others. London; New York: Routledge; 1999.
15. Salzman PC. On reflexivity. American Anthropologist 2002; 104:805–11.

16. Robertson J. Reflexivity redux: a pithy polemic on "positionality". Anthropological Quarterly 2002; 75:785–92.

17. Pillow W. Confession, catharsis, or cure? Rethinking the uses of reflexivity as methodological power in qualitative research. International Journal of Qualitative Studies in Education 2003; 16:175–96.

18. Ruby J. Exposing yourself: reflexivity, anthropology, and film. Semiotica 1980; 30:153.

19. Herzfeld M. Essentialism. In: Barnard A, Spencer J, eds. Routledge Encyclopedia of Social and Cultural Anthropology. 2nd ed. London: England; 2010.

20. Brezina V. Philosophical anthropology and philosophy in anthropology. In: Giri AK, Clammer JR, eds. Philosophy and anthropology : border crossing and transformations. New York: Anthem Press; 2013.

21. Human evolution timeline interactive. Smithsonian Institution, 2016. (Accessed March 1, 2016, at http://humanorigins.si.edu/evidence/human-evolution-timeline-interactive.)

22. Geertz C. Thick description: toward an interpretive theory of culture. The interpretation of cultures: selected essays. New York: Basic Books; 1973.

## Chapter 4

1. Lélé S, Norgaard RB. Practicing interdisciplinarity. BioScience 2005; 55:967–75.

2. Schmidt R, Smyth M, Kowalski V. Teaching the scientific literature review. Santa Barbara: ABC-CLIO; 2014.

3. Booth WC, Colomb GG, Williams JM. The craft of research. Chicago: University of Chicago Press; 1995.

4. Hubbuch SM. Writing research papers across the curriculum. Fort Worth: Harcourt Brace Jovanovich; 1992.

5. Bessire L, Bond D. Ontological anthropology and the deferral of critique. American Ethnologist 2014; 41:440–56.

# CREDITS

Page 7, *Figure 1.1*: Photograph by Gregory Bateson and reproduced from the Margaret Mead Archives, Manuscript Division, Library of Congress, Washington, D.C. Courtesy of the Institute for Intercultural Studies, Inc., New York.

Page 161, *Figure 6.1*: CALVIN AND HOBBES © 1993 Watterson. Reprinted with permission of UNIVERSAL UCLICK. All rights reserved.

# INDEX